Better Homes
and Jungles

STEVE FARRAR

To Tom
Best wishes
in the jungle
Steve Farrar

MULTNOMAH
Portland, Oregon

For speaking and conference information, write or call:

Steve Farrar
Strategic Living
P.O. Box 2001
Coppell, TX 75019
Phone (214) 393-1144

Unless otherwise indicated, all Scripture references are from the Holy Bible: New International Version, copyright 1973, 1978, 1984, by the International Bible Society. Used by permission of Zondervan Bible Publishers.

Scripture references marked KJV are from the Holy Bible: Authorized King James Version.

Scripture references marked NASB are from the New American Standard Bible, copyright the Lockman Foundation 1960, 1962, 1963, 1968, 1971, 1973, 1975, 1977. Used by permission.

Edited by Steve Halliday
Cover design by Bruce DeRoos

BETTER HOMES AND JUNGLES
©1991 by Steve Farrar
Published by Multnomah Press
10209 SE Division Street
Portland, Oregon 97266

Multnomah Press is a ministry of Multnomah School of the Bible,
8435 NE Glisan Street, Portland, Oregon 97220.

Printed in the United States of America.

Library of Congress Cataloging-in-Publication Data

Farrar, Steve.
    Better homes and jungles : vaccinate your family against creeping affluenza / Steve Farrar.
        p. cm.
    Includes bibliographical references.
    ISBN 0-99070-452-7
        1. Family—United States—Religious life. 2. Success—Religious aspects—Christianity. 3. Wealth—Religious aspects—Christianity.
    I. Title.
BV4526.2.F35 1991
248.4—dc20
                                                                91-20338
                                                                CIP

91 92 93 94 95 96 97 98 99 - 10 9 8 7 6 5 4 3 2 1

Dedication

To Beverly Farrar

In appreciation of my superb and skillful mom,
who consistently sacrificed what was best for her,
to do what was best for me.

Acknowledgments

This book has been a team effort. Any author will tell you that writing is not a one-man show. There are some key people who contributed significantly to my life as I was writing these pages. Each one helped to make this book a reality.

Thanks to the Monday morning study group: Bobby Grisham, Bryan Owens, Jeff Rogers, Bill Howard, and Dave Gustafson. Their input, comments, and evaluations were extremely helpful as this material was being shaped in the initial stages, even though some of them were riding high on caffeine that early in the morning.

A host of family and friends across the country gave valuable personal time to carefully critique and scrutinize the manuscript: Gary Rosberg, Bryan Owens, Ryon Paton, Walter Spires, Doug and Jane Anne Smith, Jeff Farrar, and my wife, Mary. Their astute observations are greatly appreciated. Each of them provided appraisals that were cogent and carefully crafted.

The Multnomah gang out in Oregon is always a delight to work with. Larry Libby and Steve Halliday are my editorial watchdogs who always bark encouragement, even when there is little to bark about. Brenda Jose is one of the most creative people I have ever met. Her innovative touch makes producing a book a whole lot of fun. And special thanks to Bruce DeRoos for his artistic flair that produced such a unique cover.

I am fortunate to have three very special children who understand that writing a book is a project that involves the entire family. I am grateful to my daughter Rachel, who spun off some very creative ideas for the book cover. John and Josh, along with Rachel, often helped me think through a multitude of possible titles and chapter headings. I am very privileged to have such gifted helpers under my own roof.

This book would not have been written without the versatility of my wife, Mary. Believe me when I say that she covers an incredible number of bases for me in order to protect my time. Mary keeps the jungle from growing over me while I am writing. She's a wise theologian, a thorough editor, and is the very best at screening phone calls. Mary has proved for fourteen years that the happiest of men are those who out-marry themselves.

Part One

The Law of the Jungle

Part Two

The Lord of the Jungle

Part One

*T*HE *L*AW OF THE *J*UNGLE

Chapter 1

Killer Mushrooms

The main emotion of the adult American
who has had all the advantages of wealth, education,
and culture is disappointment.

John Cheever

I was fine until I picked up the magazine. In fact, I was doing great. I *was* tired, because I had just finished mowing our front and back yards on a sweltering and smothering summer day. The temperature was close to 100 and the humidity was over 90 percent. I was worn out after six hours in that kind of steam bath, but as I sat down to guzzle another iced tea, I had a real feeling of accomplishment. The yard looked like a million bucks and so did our ten-year-old house with its new coat of paint. I was exhausted, but I also had a sense of contentment and satisfaction after finishing my yard and taking a look at the end product.

That is, until I picked up one of Mary's magazines lying on the coffee table. As I flipped through its pages I noticed an article about remodeling your kitchen. The story concerned a Des Moines couple who decided to redo their eleven-year-old kitchen. A full array of before and after pictures complemented the story. The finished kitchen was incredible.

I flipped a few pages over and noticed a do-it-yourself feature on putting in a deck in your back yard. I already had a deck in my back yard, but to tell you the truth, it didn't look anything like the deck in the magazine. Until I saw the article about decks, I was perfectly happy with the one I had. That very afternoon I had spent a great deal of time on my deck, taking frequent breaks from the blasting heat. In fact, I had a real sense of contentment and enjoyment on that deck as I sat drinking my iced tea under our shady, thirty-foot maple tree.

I was fine until I picked up the magazine.

Just moments before I had viewed with satisfaction the freshly mowed and edged green Bermuda grass which contrasted beautifully with the fresh vanilla white paint on our two-story house. That house looked great. As I went inside to sit down, I was filled with the all-American pride that comes from a sense of ownership. I was proud of my home and how it looked.

That is, until I picked up the magazine.

Within minutes I could hardly stomach the idea of living in such a roach trap. Just look at the kitchen! Those counter tops are *formica!*

What we need to do is to get some counter tops with ceramic tile, I thought. *This kitchen looks like something in a Roy Rogers western that got dragged on a cattle drive. We've got military personnel in Saudi Arabia eating in canvas mess halls that look better than this dump.*

And look at these cabinets! I've seen firewood that's in better shape than these cabinets. The magazine featured a pantry whose multiple shelves rotate in a circle at the touch of a button. Look at this dump we call a pantry! It's about as well-organized as the backpack of a five-year-old going off to kindergarten. There are cans of soup somewhere in there that are three or four years old. At least, I think there are. We put things in our pantry and never see them again. There's so much stuff crowded in there that we could feed a small country for several weeks. But we can't get to it. What we need are some rotating, motorized cabinets!

I was fine until I picked up the magazine.

How did I go from such satisfaction with my home to near disgust in so few minutes? The answer is comparison. You see, I was fine until I picked up the magazine.

By the way, can you guess what magazine I was reading? It has a circulation of more than 8 million. It's known as *Homes and Gardens*. No, that's not right. It's **Better Homes and Gardens.** Better than whose? Better than mine!

Think of it. Eight million people every month read this magazine. That's a lot of people. No wonder America is so driven. We're reminded every month that someone out there has something that's better. It may be a deck, it may be a house, or it may be a garden.

Some people have the space and time to cultivate a garden. I have the space, but I haven't made the time. Most people I know with gardens grow corn, peas, carrots, squash, and tomatoes. If I had a garden I would raise all of those things, as well as one other item that usually isn't found in backyard gardens. I would raise mushrooms.

I like mushrooms on my pizza. I also like fresh mushrooms in my salad. When I was a kid, I used to eat Campbell's mushroom soup for lunch. I have liked mushrooms for a long time. But there is something everyone who likes mushrooms should know. There are good mushrooms and there are bad mushrooms. And if you don't know the difference, they can kill you.

I like to be successful in life. I imagine that you do, too. I work hard to be successful in my speaking. I work hard to be successful in my writing. When I was a kid, I wanted to be a success when I grew up. But there is something everyone who likes success should know. There is good success and bad success. And if you don't know the difference, it can kill you.

I am convinced that success is a spiritual mushroom. If you get the wrong kind, it can paralyze you spiritually, callous you emotionally, and put your family relationships into a catatonic state.

If you don't think mushrooms can ruin your day, then you might be interested in reading the following:

> There are a thousand or more varieties of mushrooms that are good to eat. . . . The most dreaded of the poisonous mushrooms are two members of the Amanita group. One is the death cup, and the other is the fly amanita.
>
> The death cup grows in the woods from June until fall. Its poison acts like the venom of a rattlesnake, as it separates the corpuscles in the blood from the serum. No antidote is known for the poison of the death cup. The only hope for anyone who has eaten it is to clean out his stomach promptly with a stomach pump. It is small wonder that one variety is known as the *destroying angel*.

The death cup has often been mistaken for the common mushroom. A person should not make this mistake if he observes *carefully*. The poisonous plant has white gills, white spores, and the fatal poison cup around its stem. The plant that is safe to eat has pink gills, brown spores, and no cup. Many of the mistakes come from picking it in the button stage, for it does not show all these differences until it has grown larger."[1]

The danger in picking mushrooms is that the differences between the good and the bad mushrooms are so subtle. You must look carefully for specific color, specific shapes, and specific characteristics. The same is true of spiritual mushrooms. Make no mistake, families all around us are dying because husbands and wives have developed a craving for the wrong kind of mushrooms. They crave success mushrooms. And they are sharing them with their children.

It is no mistake that one type of mushroom is known as the destroying angel. It looks inviting, but it's a killer. If we knew how dangerous the wrong kind of success could be, we could protect ourselves and our children from the poisonous varieties. Ignorance of the difference between edible and poisonous mushrooms can kill us.

Years ago the story was told of a group of university students from Toronto who went up to Georgian Bay for a fishing trip. They hired a boat and a captain to take them out. When they were out on the water a tremendous storm arose, and the captain sat at the helm with a worried look on his face. The students made fun of him. One of the students said, "We aren't afraid. Why should you be afraid?" The captain looked at them and said, "You are too ignorant to be afraid."[2]

We can ill afford ignorance when it comes to the issue of success. Developing a healthy fear of spiritual toxins is the first step toward protecting ourselves from a wrenching and violent personal experience.

A THEOLOGY OF MUSHROOMS

Did you ever have to take castor oil when you were a kid? I remember staying with my grandmother one time when my parents went out of town. I started to come down with something and my grandmother pulled out the castor oil to conquer the affliction. That stuff borders on the abusive. I recently read that castor oil has another use—as a lubricant for jet engines. No wonder kids hate the stuff. Why didn't they just give us a teaspoon of Pennzoil?

For most of us, the term "theology" brings the same response as does castor oil. We think both theology and castor oil are unpleasant, boring, and difficult to swallow. I am convinced that theology has been given a bad rap. Theology is not only a gift from God, it is the antidote for bad mushrooms. In fact, this book is designed to be a practical theology of mushrooms. That may sound boring, but don't forget—if you can't recognize a poisonous mushroom, it can kill you.

J. I. Packer is an expert on spiritual mushrooms. Please read his words carefully and thoughtfully, rolling them around your intellectual taste buds until you experience all of the robust and exquisite flavor:

> . . . All theology is also spirituality, in the sense that it has an influence, good or bad, positive or negative, on its recipients' relationship or lack of relationship to God. If our theology does not quicken the conscience and soften the heart, it actually hardens both; if it does not encourage the commitment of faith, it reinforces the detachment of unbelief; if it fails to promote humility, it inevitably feeds pride.
>
> So one who theologizes in public, whether formally in the pulpit, on the podium or in print, or informally from the armchair, must think hard about the effect his thoughts will have on people: God's people, and other people. Theologians are called to be the church's water engineers and sewage officers; it is their job to see that God's pure truth flows abundantly where it is needed, and to filter out any intrusive pollution that might damage health."[3]

I think Dr. Packer would agree that theology was given not only to help us enjoy clean water, but good mushrooms. The value of theology is that it will protect us from toxins and enable us to enjoy the pleasures of good mushrooms for years to come.

Spiritual mushrooms can be confusing. Success can be very good . . . but it can also be sin. You can't get through high school, let alone college, without ambition, but ambition can also be deadly to everything that is good and noble. There is a world of difference between suitable ambition and selfish ambition. Money is another spiritual mushroom. There is nothing wrong with having money, even vast sums of money. But there is everything wrong with *loving* money.

A case could be made that Solomon was the wealthiest man in history. Solomon could have bought out Donald Trump's bankers with petty cash. Solomon had spiritual mushrooms on his mind when he wrote, "He who loves money will not be satisfied with money, nor he who loves abundance with its income" (Ecclesiastes 5:10, NASB). This is why wisdom is imperative when you handle mushrooms. They are potential killers, so potent that eventually they even got Solomon. And he literally wrote the book on discerning mushrooms.

Only a novice would pick up a mushroom indiscriminately. And a foolish novice is usually a dead novice. Theology is a non-negotiable if the novice is to keep from becoming a dead novice. The Scriptures (the source of our theology) help us to discern the different types of spiritual mushrooms.

Success is one spiritual mushroom, ambition is another. Pride is also a spiritual mushroom. In chapter 2, we will take a close look at these three spiritual mushrooms. And in chapter 4 we will investigate the mushroom of money. Thus far, we have made the following distinctions:

Safe Mushrooms	*Toxic Mushrooms*
Credible Success	Cultural Success
Suitable Ambition	Selfish Ambition
Decent Pride	Deadly Pride
Using Money	Loving Money

There is one other mushroom we have not discussed. This one will surprise you. It is a fairly recent hybrid and seems to grow primarily in America. It is the mushroom of commuting.

A THEOLOGY OF COMMUTING: PART I

Tom Joyner is successful. He is at the top of his profession. His annual compensation is somewhere in the range of $600,000 to 700,000. At the age of forty, there is no question that he has made it as one of the top disc jockeys in the country. But there's something unique about Joyner. It's not the fact that he's a top-rated disc jockey in Dallas that makes him unique, but the fact that he's a top-rated deejay in Dallas . . . *and* Chicago. Tom Joyner is in the studio in Dallas every morning and in the studio in Chicago every afternoon.

Since October of 1985, Joyner has been the only disc jockey in America to have two daily radio programs in two major cities. Some people have long commutes, but this guy commutes two thousand miles round trip *every day*.

The *Dallas Morning News* recently spotlighted a day in the life of this successful entertainment figure:

> Shortly before 5:30 A.M., Joyner comes on the air at K104 in Dallas to do his 3$^1/_2$ hour morning drive time show. Shortly after 9:00 A.M., he is quickly on his way to Dallas-Ft. Worth International Airport. He goes directly to the gate, flashes his $150,000 American Airlines Airpass, and sits down in First Class seat 4A of Flight 360 to Chicago. He carries with him only his briefcase and his lunch.

> Approximately two hours later, a limo picks him up at O'Hare airport, rushes him to a local health club for a quick work out, and then dashes him to the studios of WGCI where he's on the air in Chicago from 2:00 to 6:00 for the afternoon commute crowd. Then it's a sprint back to O'Hare to catch his flight to Dallas. He touches down at DFW around 9:00 and is in bed by 11:00. And then he's up the next morning by 3:30 A.M. to do it all over again.[4]

And you thought you had a tough schedule!

How in the world can anyone keep up that kind of brutal regimen? That's almost as bad as double days in football—practice in the morning and practice in the afternoon. Do you remember those days of dragging your tortured and wounded body back into the locker room after lunch? You were so sore you could hardly pull your pads on.

"What helps," Joyner says, "is the number of flights American offers between the two cities, a strict diet, exercise and a mind-set that 'I can't get stressed out over nothing I can't control' like flight delays."[5]

So that explains how he does it. But why would anyone *want* to keep such a punishing workload? It's interesting that

his peers describe him as near fanatical about planning for his family's future. He negotiates nothing but multiyear, guaranteed contracts and commands $250,000 to $300,000 at WGCI and slightly less at K104, according to several sources.

He pockets another $100,000 or so for the syndicated urban-music countdown show titled, appropriately enough, "On The Move," a three hour weekly radio program he was handpicked to host.

Commercial endorsements: McDonald's (which he can't eat); Miller Beer (which he can't drink); and 7-Eleven, among others, give him more financial security. . . .

Joyner, who has two teenage sons, says that if there's a downside to his success, it's too little family time. "I've always worried about my responsibility as a good father and husband," says Joyner. He says it pains him to miss parent-teacher meetings, football games, and spending time with his wife.[6]

Tom Joyner is obviously a driven man. What is it that drives someone who makes $250,000 on one job to work another in a city one thousand miles away to pick up another quarter million? And then on top of all that, to work weekends to pick up another $100,000? I don't know about you, but I'm beginning to smell some mushrooms. Bad mushrooms.

COMMUTING FOR SUCCESS: PART II

I am a native Californian. Until several years ago, I had always lived in California (except for stints out of state for graduate school). I have traveled all over California. I know the way to San Jose but I did not know the way to Moreno Valley. Not only did I not know where it was, I had never heard of it. I didn't know if it was in northern California or southern California or Nebraska. I was amazed to recently read that Moreno Valley is the fastest growing city in Riverside County, California. I didn't even know it existed. But neither did a lot of other native Californians. Moreno Valley, a city just east of Riverside with a population of 116,000, scarcely had any inhabitants a decade ago.

It's an odd city, with few parks, no skating rinks, not a single miniature golf course. Until this month,it didn't even have a hospital. . . . The community is distinguished mainly by its tidy succession of one-story houses, and, of course, by the procession of young working couples heading off to their jobs in the morning and back at home at night. The nearest major employment centers are Orange County, 45 miles to the west, and Los Angeles, 70 miles northwest. The drive to L.A. takes two hours on a good day, three when an accident ties up traffic on the Pomona Freeway. It is not unusual for a resident of Moreno Valley to commute 4 to 6 hours each weekday.[7]

There is really only one reason that people would choose to live so far from where they work: affordable housing. The average home in Orange County costs $239,671; in L.A. it's $225,600; but in Moreno Valley it's $146,225.

For those of you who live in parts of the country where the housing market is more sane, it may be hard to think of a three bedroom, two bath, tract home with less than 1900 square feet for nearly $150,000 as a "bargain." But in California it's a steal. Anyone who lives in California can tell you that *successful* people own their own homes. They don't rent.

Even though the market has recently taken a drop, true believers know it will come back. Real estate is the official religion of California. And the bargain prices in Moreno Valley are enough of a steal to motivate thousands of people to commute at least four hours a day every Monday through Friday.

But there's a definite downside to home ownership, even in California. According to the *Wall Street Journal,* because of the hours it takes to go back and forth to work, residents have precious little time in which to enjoy the homes they wanted so much to own. The Reverend Gerald DeLuney, parish priest of St. Christopher's Church in Moreno Valley, worries that "family life has been killed" by the commuting and the struggle to meet mortgage payments.

Psychiatrist Daniel Amen, who counsels a number of these commuting families, sees in them "physical and mental deterioration, including anxiety disorders, tension, chronic headaches and diarrhea. One woman, who with her husband has commuted for seven years, admits that 'she gets sick a lot and suffers depression' about the fact that she doesn't get to be with her family. A major worry is all the time she must be away from her two-year-old daughter. 'When she was little, I had this fear she wouldn't recognize me. . . . She would be with a stranger nine, ten, eleven hours a day.' These days, she doesn't get to see her little girl in the morning before she leaves for work, but she thinks of her often during the day."[8]

This same woman confesses that the long commute she and her husband take "has hurt her family, her health and her self-esteem." But they own a home, so they are successful. And it's killing them. Bad mushrooms can do that. Perhaps we should update our list.

Safe Mushrooms	Toxic Mushrooms
Credible Success	Cultural Success
Suitable Ambition	Selfish Ambition
Decent Pride	Deadly Pride
Using Money	Loving Money
Usual Commuting	Ultra-Commuting

More and more families move into Moreno Valley every day. I'm sure that most of them plan to be very happy. They own their own homes in California and that means they've climbed another rung on the ladder of success. But they may be getting less than they bargained for.

The problem is this: you can buy a house, but you can't buy a home. And happiness is only found in homes. Most of these folks haven't found that out . . . yet. It's like George Bernard Shaw once observed: "There are two sources of unhappiness in life. One is not getting what you want; the other is getting it."

When you buy a new house from a builder, it comes with a warranty which covers any possible defects. You can get a warranty for a house, but you can't get one for a home. Houses are built with brick and mortar. Homes are built with the harmonious interactions of husbands, wives, and children committed to each other. But you have to be there to interact. It's obvious from all of the growth that there are a lot of houses in Moreno Valley. It's too bad there aren't more homes.

You may be asking yourself what would drive someone (no pun intended) to commute a minimum of two hours in the morning and two hours back home again in the evening, whether by car or by plane. That is four *hours* every day. Four hours traveling to and from work when you only have twenty four hours in a day. Think of it. That's one-sixth of your life, not working, but going to work. That's nuts! That's crazy! That's . . . that's . . . idiotic! Precisely.

THE IDIOT SAVANT

Dustin Hoffman is a gifted actor. He can take any role and almost make you forget that he is Dustin Hoffman. He is a superb craftsman, whether the role calls for the comedy of *Tootsie* or the suspense and anguish of having his cavities drilled without Novocain in *Marathon Man.*

Many think Hoffman outdid himself in *Rain Man.* In *Rain Man*, Hoffman was asked to play a role completely out of character. To put it bluntly, Hoffman was asked to play the part of an idiot.

Lest you misunderstand, I am talking about the kind of idiot defined in the *Oxford English Dictionary:* "a person so deficient in mental or intellectual faculty, as to be incapable of ordinary acts of reasoning or rational conduct." To call someone an "idiot" is an inhumane thing to do, especially if you have ever been with people who truly suffer with idiocy.

As a freshman in college I spent a day with other students visiting a mental institution in Northern California. By mistake, we were taken into a section of the hospital the general public is normally not allowed to visit. There I saw people so deficient in mental faculties as to be incapable of ordinary reasoning or rational conduct. It was shocking to see hapless people unable to function in the most elementary ways. For their own protection, they had to be watched constantly. In the true and most tragic sense of the word, these people were idiots.

It is important to understand, however, that Hoffman was not playing the part of what the Oxford dictionary would define as an idiot. To be exact, Hoffman was playing an "idiot savant." There is a pivotal difference.

The savant syndrome . . . is an exceedingly rare condition in which persons with serious mental handicaps have spectacular islands of intelligence, *even genius*, in a sea of mental instability.[9]

This explains why idiot savants can do extraordinary feats that "normal" people could never hope to duplicate. These idiots are certified geniuses. Although the mental handicaps of idiot savants severely impair their ability to adapt to surroundings and to relate to other people, they are uniquely and extraordinarily gifted in a particular area.

What other explanation could there be for how one young blind woman can run through a thickly wooded forest, instinctively avoiding the trees she cannot see? Although she is incapable of holding a normal conversation, she has an astonishing spatial sense.

This same girl can "sing any song after hearing it once and has memorized whole musicals, playing them back on the piano." Some idiot savants can flawlessly play entire movements of classical music after hearing them for the first time.

The idiot savant has a "narrow range of skills: a flair for music or the visual arts, mathematical ability, mechanical wizardry, or mnemonic skills such as calendar calculation (divining instantly the day of the week a particular date will fall in a given year)."[10] The character Hoffman played in *Rain Man* could instantly calculate the numbers at Las Vegas gambling tables—yet couldn't find his way to the parking lot without assistance.

In layman's terms, an idiot savant is a severely mentally handicapped person who has an extraordinary ability to do one or two things astonishingly well, whether it be playing a Mozart concerto after hearing it just once or instantaneously figuring the annual interest on the national debt.

Do you remember our definition of the savant syndrome? "The savant syndrome . . . is an exceedingly rare condition in which persons with serious mental handicaps have spectacular islands of intelligence, *even genius*, in a sea of mental instability."

THE AMERICAN CORPORATE IDIOT SAVANT

Another type of person is much more common in America than the idiot savant. Although this type numbers in the hundreds of thousands, if not millions, it is not recognized as a handicapped group. Unfortunately, these people are often held up as role models to be followed and emulated. They sometimes make appearances on the cover of *Forbes* magazine. They are the American corporate idiot savants—people who suffer from crippling disorders in the spiritual and relational dimensions of their lives. Yet when it comes to their careers, they are able to do amazing feats. Let's note several characteristics of this spiritual disorder that over the last two decades has reached epidemic proportions.

1. The corporate idiot savant is handicapped relationally and spiritually.

This syndrome is exceedingly common. Those afflicted seek and, at times, display spectacular islands of success and accomplishment, even genius, in a sea of relational and spiritual instability.

These people are very good at "making it." While they are extraordinarily gifted at climbing the corporate ladder, they usually need assistance in getting home at night. They are so preoccupied with career that they lack energy for anything else, including relationships. They are committed to professional excellence, period. Intimate and significant relationships with spouses, children, and friends, along with any possibility of spiritual growth, are sacrificed daily on the altar located left of the entrance to corporate headquarters.

> James Patterson and Peter Kim set out to take the moral pulse of America in the 1990s. Using state-of-the-art research techniques that go way beyond superficial five-minute polls, they conducted the largest survey of private morals ever undertaken in any country to unearth and quantify the personal ethics, values, and beliefs of our time. . . . The results, which vary widely from region to region, are nothing less than astonishing.[11]

Patterson and Kim found 2000 men and women who agreed to answer 1800 questions in complete anonymity. One of their findings considered personal truthfulness. Here's what they found:

> Lying has become an integral part of the American culture, a trait of the American character. We lie and don't even think about it.

We lie for no reason. The writer Vance Bourjaily once said, "Like most men, I tell a hundred lies a day." That's about right. And the people we lie to most are those closest to us.[12]

Their study found that 56 percent of the men and 35 percent of the women felt that it was OK to lie to keep a job. There is nothing that erodes relationships faster than lying. Yet many are willing to sacrifice personal integrity and healthy relationships for the opportunity of taking another step toward the top.

2. The corporate idiot savant tends to use people.

These people are good with goals and objectives, but poor with people. They are severely handicapped in their most meaningful personal relationships. They are able to deal with people and, in some cases, are adept at interacting with people, but they can only do so at a superficial level. Many of them are masters at manipulating people without those people realizing what is happening. When it comes to relationships, they are a mile wide and one inch deep. They use people as one would use pawns in a chess game, for they are often more than willing to sacrifice a relationship in order to achieve a carefully calculated objective.

> Lord, I size up other people,
>> in terms of what they can do for me;
>> how they can further my program,
>>> feed my ego,
>>> satisfy my needs,
>>> give me strategic advantage.
> I exploit people,
>> ostensibly for your sake,
>> but really for my own sake.
> Lord, I turn to you
>> to get the inside track
>> and obtain special favors,
>>> your direction for my schemes,
>>> your power for my projects,
>>> your sanction for my ambitions,
>>> your blank checks for whatever I want.[13]

I was drawn to this prayer by Robert Raines as soon as I saw it. At one time or another, I have displayed all the tendencies of the corporate savant. I have seen the damage this syndrome can bring about. I believe I am a "recovering" corporate idiot savant. But I sure don't have this wired. That's why I look for its symptoms in my life every day.

3. The corporate idiot savant tends to love things.

The corporate idiot savant loves things and uses people. He's got it turned around. Satisfaction in life comes from loving people and using things. This is where he needs help.

Part of the problem is that corporate idiot savants have the extraordinary ability to spot mushrooms at great distances. Unfortunately, they are not able to distinguish between edible mushrooms and hazardous ones. They are particularly fond of certain kinds of mushrooms found in the success family of spiritual mushrooms, namely *Americus Mercedus, Americus Rolexus,* and two Japanese hybrids, *Americus Lexus* and *Americus Infinitius.*

This is not to say that everyone who enjoys these particular types of *Americus* mushrooms is without discernment or is out of balance. There are those who enjoy the *Americus* variety of mushrooms and yet most definitely are not American corporate idiot savants. The difference is this: *the telling characteristic of American corporate idiot savants is that they will sacrifice almost anything they have, including their families and their marriages, to obtain greater quantities of the* Americus *mushroom.* They are as addicted to success as the miserable creatures writhing in the alley behind a crack house. Their craving for things is insatiable.

A case in point is Robert Jacoby, former president of Sunrise Savings and Loan (now insolvent) who stated, "I have a pretty wife, a Jaguar, a Mercedes, a beautiful home, and a yacht. I want a Ferrari, a bigger house, and a bigger boat." With an attitude like that, how secure do you think his wife feels?

Alexander Solzhenitsyn poignantly notes that "the constant desire to have still more things and still a better life and the struggle to obtain them imprints many Western faces with worry and even depression, though it is customary to conceal such feelings." Corporate idiot savants are good at that.

4. The corporate idiot savant has a narrow vocabulary.

Some institutionalized idiot savants are so handicapped they are unable to communicate. Others, like the young man who Hoffman portrayed, are more fortunate. They can communicate with a limited and elementary vocabulary.

The American corporate idiot savant also has a limited vocabulary, consisting almost exclusively of words that begin with the letter A. The following vocabulary list includes words commonly used by American corporate idiot savants. There is nothing inherently wrong with *most* of the words in this list. However, most corporate idiot savants are *preoccupied* with one or more of the following words, thus leading them into excessive and out-of-balance lifestyles. Some of these favorite words are:

Achievement	Acquisition	Advancement	Action
Ability	Arrival	Attainment	Aspiring
Ambitious	Aggressive	Adequate	Assertive
Arrogant	Accomplish	Appearance	Accumulate

It should be noted again that the corporate idiot savant's fatal flaw is his preoccupation with this vocabulary list; it costs him some of the most significant and wonderful pleasures life has to offer. The corporate idiot savant is convinced that happiness lies in realizing the list. But he is often disappointed. I think George Gilder said it best:

> Men lust, but they know not what for;
> They wander, and lose track of the goal;
> They fight and compete, but they forget the prize;
> They spread seed, but spurn the seasons of growth;
> They chase power and glory, and miss the meaning of life.[14]

A THEOLOGY OF BASKETBALL

Two years ago, I was in the back yard shooting baskets with my son, Josh. Josh was five then, and hadn't really mastered the fundamentals of the game. Josh would dribble once or twice and then pick up the ball and take twenty or thirty steps before making a shot. That's OK when you're five.

A few minutes later, Rachel, who was then ten, came out and

joined in. Before you knew it, my eight-year-old, John, had joined us, and we had ourselves a full-fledged game. Then my wife Mary came out and got into the action. We were all there: shooting, passing, rebounding, and traveling.

Every thirty seconds or so, Josh would get the ball, forget to dribble, and run thirty or forty yards for a touchdown. When you're five, it's hard to remember what game you're playing. We were laughing and yelling and having a great time, and then the ball bounced off of Rachel's foot and went under the deck. It took John about 45 seconds to crawl under the deck and retrieve the ball.

While I waited for him to get the ball, suddenly something unexpected happened. It's hard to explain, but it was as though time suddenly stood still and everything around me froze. For some reason, I saw everything before me through the lens of eternity. Through this lens, everything took on a different perspective. I saw Josh hugging Mary's leg, I saw Rachel telling John to hurry up and get the ball, and in the quietness of my heart I paused and thought, *You know, Steve, it doesn't get any better than this.*

You've seen the beer commercial a hundred times. Several guys are fly fishing in a cool, clear mountain stream somewhere in Idaho. At the end of a long day of catching scores of trout, they sit around the glowing campfire and finish their charbroiled meal. Then one turns to his buddies and declares, "Guys, it doesn't get any better than this."

I've got news for that guy. As much fun as that would be, it does get better than that. It gets better when:

• you have a personal relationship with Jesus Christ and you *know* that He is overseeing all the events of your life, including your career;

• you have a husband and wife who accept one another, love one another, forgive one another, encourage one another, and occasionally shoot baskets together;

• you make time to be with your kids and enjoy the fun of just being together . . . you take time to shoot baskets, to play that board game, to go to the science fair, to ride around one evening before Christmas and look at all the Christmas lights.

That evening, as I stood in the back yard and looked at my family, it hit me like a ton of bricks. *This* is success. *This* is happiness. I have been given the gift of a family and we belong to Jesus Christ. It doesn't get any better than that. And I realized it just by shooting baskets in the back yard with my family.

One day in the future, when I am seventy or seventy-five years old, I'll be sitting around the table with Mary, drinking a glass of iced tea on a beautiful spring evening, and I'll say to her, "Do you remember when we used to play basketball with the kids in the back yard? Weren't those great days?" And we'll pass the evening together, thinking of the days that we are living *now*.

The point is this: in another thirty-five years, I will be remembering the quality of our relationships. Not the things we had or didn't have, but the love and fun and tears and yelling in the back yard. That's what I'll remember.

What will you remember in another thirty-five years? I wish we had theaters where parents could gaze into the future and witness what their lives would be like in three or four decades. I wish I could get them to see what's ahead: pitiful scenes of lonely, shriveled, abandoned old people whose kids couldn't care less if they were alive or dead. I wish I could hand them visual evidence of what bad mushrooms can do. But I can't.

The best I can do is to point to the Bible and testify to how its message has blessed and enriched and directed my own family. By God's grace, in thirty-five years Mary and I will look back and rejoice in the love and satisfaction we receive from our family. I pray our kids will be able to do the same.

That's true success. That is true happiness. That's better homes and gardens. It's literally in your own back yard. That's where the good mushrooms tend to grow. And you don't have to commute four hours to get there.

Notes

1. *World Book Encyclopedia*, "Mushrooms," II (Chicago: Field Enterprises, 1959), 534.

2. Steve Brown, *No More Mr. Nice Guy* (Nashville: Thomas Nelson, 1986), 132.

3. J. I. Packer, *A Quest For Godliness* (Wheaton: Crossway, 1990), 15.

4. "Pilot of the Airwaves," *Dallas Morning News*, 17 October 1990, Today Section, 1.

5. Ibid.

6. Ibid.

7. "What's News," *Wall Street Journal*, 25 October 1990, 1.

8. Ibid.

9. *Omni*, September 1989, 10.

10. Ibid., 10.

11. James Patterson and Peter Kim, *The Day America Told the Truth* (New York: Prentice Hall, 1991), jacket copy.

12. Ibid., 7.

13. Robert Raines, quoted in Kent Hughes, *Liberating Ministry* (Wheaton: Tyndale, 1988).

14. George Gilder, cited by Tom L. Eisenman, *Temptations Men Face* (Downer's Grove: InterVarsity Press, 1990), 33.

Chapter 2

IN THE JUNGLE THE LION SLEEPS TONIGHT

Every morning I get up and look through the Forbes *list of the richest people in America. If I'm not there, I go to work.*

Robert Orben

Tarzan was not himself. And Jane was worried. It was apparent Tarzan was developing a problem. A very serious problem. For the last several days, the pattern was the same. Tarzan would come home after work and pour himself a double shot of Scotch.

This made no sense. Tarzan was very conscious of his health—he watched his diet, played racquetball several times a week, and rarely touched desserts. He never touched alcohol. That's why Jane knew something was wrong. Something was behind this new bout of drinking. Jane knew she had to say something. After several days, she finally did.

"Tarzan," she said, "I'm concerned about your drinking. Every evening you come home and immediately look for the liquor. That's not like you. And it's a very bad example for Boy."

Tarzan dropped his head and was silent. Finally he said, "Jane, you're exactly right. This has got to stop. There's only one problem."

"What's that?" Jane asked.

"It's a jungle out there."

I agree with Tarzan. It *is* a jungle out there. A jungle can be a dangerous place to live, even if your jungle doesn't have lions and tigers. All a jungle needs to be dangerous is a couple of freeways and a corporate ladder. Just take a look at Gary.

Gary is a thirty-nine-year-old executive moving on the fast track. He has just entered his nearly barren apartment after another long day at the office . . . striding across the living room he flicks on the TV to catch what's left of the 11:00 o'clock news. He peels off his jacket and tie, grabs a cold bottle of Molson's from the near-empty refrigerator, and sprawls across the sofa, pushing aside some newspapers.

Relaxing now for the first time that day, Gary takes a look around the room and reminds himself *again* that he'd better get some more furniture and fix the place up. Divorced for almost a year, his apartment still has a warehouse flavor . . . *Too much excitement at work right now. Just don't have the time. I've got the opportunity of a lifetime and I'm not about to get sidetracked and blow it.*

A smirk comes over Gary's face. He's thinking about his successful put-down and humiliation of an office rival earlier that day at a meeting with top executives of his division. He can do it good, all right. And with finesse; like a knife through butter. Nothing crude about this guy.

They know him at the office as hard-working and very aggressive. Savvy about the ins and outs of the system, and always ready to lunge for the next project or opportunity that comes along. A real go-for-it man. But that's only part of the picture. He is playing a high-stakes game in an organization that has a destructively competitive environment at the top, where everyone is constantly maneuvering to do each other in as they try to climb higher and higher.

Soon the sound of the TV anchorman fades as Gary drifts off to sleep, where he encounters an old companion: a recurring dream of walking down a long, empty corridor in his office building. As he walks along he feels mounting tension, and each time he passes an office doorway he strikes a karate pose, anticipating some unseen attacker. Eventually he passes a door to the stairway. It springs open. Standing there is a person wearing a frogman's suit and mask. The figure points a speargun at Gary. Without saying a word, he fires it at Gary's heart. In slow motion, Gary watches it penetrate his chest and feels it tearing into his beating heart, which pours forth great torrents of blood. And then he wakes up screaming.[1]

It *is* a jungle out there. Tarzan used to swing through the jungle and scream as he went, but this guy is screaming in his jungle for a different reason. Excuse me while I do a Jesse Jackson imitation, but it's stressful to be successful. This guy is obviously stressed as he goes about his jungle. But he's not the only one who's stressed.

Recently, an advertising salesman needed medical treatment after he screamed so loudly in an argument with his boss that he punctured a lung. Another patient, an office receptionist, suffered such stress-induced vomiting that she had to quit her job. And a third, a Wall Street broker being treated for hypertension, was so certain his death was imminent that he refused to take his children to the park for fear that they would be abandoned when he died.[2]

Another man describes his situation this way: "You know, it's a real jungle out there. I mean, sometimes my office is a zoo. Just when I think I've finally got it made and get some respect, along comes someone else to challenge my authority. I feel stressed all the time, trying to keep my position and worrying about others trying to get what I've got."[3]

The evidence supports the premise. It's stressful to be successful.

THE PRESSURE TO BE SUCCESSFUL

Why are so many stressed out? People feel a tremendous pressure to be successful, to make it, to get ahead of the pack. No one is willing to be ordinary. Terry Hershey writes, "We live in a world where more is never enough. Coping mechanisms and consequences are evident. We cannot be content, so we fantasize about those who do 'arrive' by reading about lifestyles of rich and famous people; we sacrifice the values of our 'ordinary life' of relationships, family and personal solitude to pursue the ecstasy that will let us 'be somebody.' "[4]

Hershey points out that the media says: "If you're living life right, you're in ecstasy most of the time." And the only way to have a shot at ecstasy is to have the right career. Without the right career, it is nearly impossible to get your ticket to success, significance, and serious income.

A Denver attorney recently put it like this: "Our professions have become very important to us and we're willing to perhaps sacrifice other things for them: marriages, families, free time, relaxation. Our marriages seem like mergers, our divorces like divestitures. [I have] gone through a number of important relationships which have failed because my commitment to my job was greater than my commitment to the relationship. If it was a tossup between getting the deal done and coming home for supper, the deal got done."[5]

Let's face it. There are times when everyone has to stay late. That's not the issue this guy is talking about. He is endorsing a lifestyle that *consistently and purposefully* chooses career and business over personal relationships. If you're going to be successful, the reasoning goes, sacrificing spouses and children is the cost of doing business. Why would anyone be willing to make such sacrifices? The answer is simple. Our culture believes that there is only one place to find true happiness, and that place is called Success.

Anthony Campolo has written that "success is a shining city, a pot of gold at the end of the rainbow. We dream of it as children, we strive for it through our adult lives, and we suffer melancholy in old age if we have not reached it. *Success in the place of happiness.* And the anxieties we suffer at the thought of not arriving there give us ulcers, heart attacks, and nervous disorders. If our reach exceeds our grasp, and we fail to achieve what we want, life seems meaningless and we feel emotionally dead."[6]

That's why we are so stressed out. That's why we are so pressured. We can live with almost anything except the thought of not being successful. And it's killing us.

A DEFINITION OF SUCCESS

Success is a hard word to nail down. It means so many different things to different people.

G. K. Chesterton had this to say about success: "To begin with, of course, there is no such thing as Success. Or, if you like to put it so, there is nothing that is not successful. That a thing is successful merely means that it is; a millionaire is successful in being a millionaire and a donkey in being a donkey. Any live man has succeeded in living; any dead man may have succeeded in committing suicide."[7]

Success is indeed a strange word. Some definitions are highly positive, others are just as negative. It reminds me of how we use the word "love." I love my wife and kids. I love to see Joe Montana get the ball back with less than two minutes left in the game with the 49ers down by four points. I love the ribs at Powdrell's Bar-B-Que in Albuquerque. I'd love to drop twenty pounds and keep it off.

When we use the word love so loosely, it tends to lose its bite. The word *love* has become an acceptable substitute for the word *like*. I love my wife and kids, but I like to see Montana get the ball with two minutes left. I like Bar B barbecued ribs and if I didn't like them so much (and the potato salad) I could probably drop that extra weight.

My point is this: There is a legitimate use of the word love and a cheapened usage. The same goes for success. In my opinion, there are two kinds of success. One is good and healthy, what I call *credible* success. The other is poisonous and dangerous. I call it *cultural* success.

Cultural Success

John Johnston has managed to capture the subtleties of what the average American would recognize as "success."

According to Johnston: "Success is attaining cultural goals that are sure to elevate one's perceived importance within that culture. In practical terms, it means an elevation in power (having commands obeyed and wishes granted); privilege (being given special rights or favors); or wealth (accumulating financial reserves and the accompanying security)."[8]

Let's make a few observations about this definition of *cultural* success.

1. Success is attaining cultural goals.

What passes for success in corporate America probably wouldn't have much meaning in Mozambique. Cultural success can be finally attaining a corner office, or a parking space with your name on it, or sitting at the head table at a company function.

But for someone outside the culture, there's not much difference if your office is in the middle of the floor or on the corner. They probably aren't going to be overwhelmed by the fact that you have a tiny space of asphalt with your name stenciled over it, or by the fact that you sat at a long table in a hotel ballroom facing everyone else. But in our culture, those things can be very significant. But remember, they are only significant in our culture.

It's something like what Coach John McKay of USC said to his team after they had been humiliated 51-0 by Notre Dame. McKay came into the locker room and saw a group of beaten, worn-out, and thoroughly depressed young football players who were not accustomed to losing. He stood up on a bench and said, "Men, let's keep this in perspective. There are 800 million Chinese who don't even know this game was played." That's what you call perspective.

2. Attaining cultural goals elevates one's perceived importance.

Note that success doesn't elevate your importance. It elevates your *perceived* importance. A lot of business people use the American Express card. It can be a handy tool, especially when you are on the road (or so the advertising would lead us to believe). For years, the American Express card came in only one color: green. It was like what Henry Ford used to say about the Model T: It comes in any color you want, as long as it's black.

Then one day American Express introduced the Gold Card, marketed to those who desired to climb a step above the herd that carried the green card. The gold also came with a higher annual fee, although the services rendered were basically the same.

They didn't stop there. After hundreds of thousands of green card members upgraded to the gold, they had to go another step. So they came out with the platinum American Express card. This is only available to the top 2 percent of American Express customers. For the privilege of paying for dinner with platinum instead of green or gold, you shell out an annual fee of $300.

Why would anyone care about having a green card that costs $35, a gold card that costs $75, or a platinum card that goes for $300 a year? The answer is simple: perceived importance. When you lay down a platinum card to pay for your business meal, your client is going to be impressed that you had the financial assets necessary to qualify for such a privilege (or he's going to think you're nuts for spending $300 for a plastic card that you could have picked up for $35). Obviously, the person who has plunked down $300 for the platinum is counting on the fact that those who see him pull platinum out of his wallet will be impressed. That's perceived importance.

3. Success is an elevation in power.

Power is having your commands obeyed and your wishes granted. As one makes his way up the corporate ladder, more and more power will be accrued. It can be used for good or bad, depending upon the character of the individual.

In 1853, Cornelius Vanderbilt had a fortune estimated at $220 million which was invested to yield 25 percent a year. In this same year, at the age of 59, Vanderbilt took the first vacation of his life. While he was touring Europe in a custom-built steamship, he got word that two of his associates were challenging his power while he was gone. Vanderbilt immediately shot off a letter: "Gentlemen, you have undertaken to cheat me. I won't sue you, for the law is too slow. I'll ruin you."[9]

As you climb higher and higher on the ladder, you will find yourself wielding more power. Power can become an addiction all by itself. It is difficult to climb the ladder and use your power wisely. All too often, as Lyman Bryson has observed, "The qualities that get a man into power are not those that lead him, once established, to use power wisely."

4. Success is an elevation in privilege.

As one becomes more and more successful, the more privileges one enjoys. It may begin with a company car, followed by the corner office, then the key to the executive washroom and dining room, then access to the company's luxury box to watch the local NBA team. Success always involves increasing privileges. That's what makes success so inviting. There's nothing wrong with enjoying a privilege. The danger is getting to the point where you expect, and even demand, the privileges.

Speaking of privilege, wouldn't it be nice to have a little time off in Paris? I recently came across a real deal on plane tickets that might interest you.

Between January 1, 1991 through March 31, 1991 you can save $1,956 on the Concorde to Paris. By purchasing a roundtrip first-class ticket on Air France using the American Express card, Air

France will allow you to experience the Concorde between New York and Paris. The regular fare on the Concorde roundtrip is $11,700. This special first-class fare on Air France is just $9,744, a savings of $1,956 roundtrip. For full details call Air France at 1-800-232-2557.

With a deal like that, I bet the phone lines are jammed. But I have one question. Why would a person who could afford to pay $9,744 for a plane ride need a toll-free number? I guess it's just another privilege.

5. Success is an elevation in wealth.

Wealth is defined as accumulating financial reserves and security. The higher one climbs on the corporate ladder the better the money and the benefits.

Recently, I received a nice brochure in the mail inviting me to order a set of tapes on the topic of "executive self-improvement." A graphic on the very first page of the report immediately caught my eye. It was a sketch of a pyramid that had been sectioned into parts, accompanied by a well-written and persuasive "management report."[10]

Readers were invited to look at the pyramid and decide at which level they would most likely fit. Then came this paragraph: "Most people are motivated to take the course because they are *dissatisfied* with their status in life. They are in the middle or bottom of the *earning* pyramid, and they long to move up a notch or two. What most people don't realize until they take the course is that they have the capability of moving to the very top! Consider your own position for a moment. Where are you now, and where would you like to be? Do you believe you can reach the very top . . . that you can *earn* more than 95 percent of the rest of the population?"

WHERE DO YOU STAND?

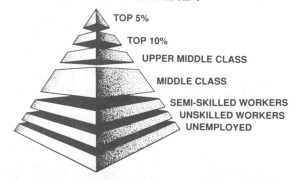

TOP 5%

TOP 10%

UPPER MIDDLE CLASS

MIDDLE CLASS

SEMI-SKILLED WORKERS
UNSKILLED WORKERS
UNEMPLOYED

Whoever came up with this pyramid is a master of human psychology. This chart is designed to do one thing: to make you discontent. Most people I know would appreciate having an income level characterized as "upper-middle." In this day and age "upper-middle" would be in the $100,000 range. But the guy making $100,000 on this pyramid is just barely above the middle! How do you think that makes him feel?

Each year, *Business Week* publishes a special issue titled "The Corporate Elite." It is "a composite picture of the Chiefs of the 1000 most valuable U.S. companies . . . In 1989 which is covered in this year's survey, the average salary for the 1,000 chiefs was a robust $841,000, up a modest 7% from 1988's $787,000." They're probably safely in the top 10 percent. Maybe if they listen to these tapes they could break into the top 5 percent and *really* be successful.

Supposedly, Donald Trump got to the top. He got to a place where he earned more than 95 percent of the population. Trump made it to the top of the pyramid. Trump was so successful at making money that he wrote a best-selling autobiography aptly titled *The Art of the Deal*.

The inside cover introduces the book this way: "Here is America's most glamorous young tycoon: the face on the covers of *Fortune, Business Week*, and *The New York Times Magazine*, the phenomenon interviewed on *60 Minutes*, today's hottest deal maker, Donald J. Trump." The back cover reads: "I don't do it for the money. *I've got enough, much more than I'll ever need*. I do it to do it. Deals are my art form" (italics mine).[11]

In 1987, Trump thought he had enough money. So did his bankers. They were both wrong. In 1989, Donald Trump had a net worth of $1.7 billion. In 1990, his net worth is zero. Now Donald has more debt than he'll ever need. So much for life at the top of the pyramid.

If you take a close look at the top of a pyramid, you will see it is a very narrow and precarious piece of real estate. It is called an apex. There is barely enough room to put both feet down securely. Perhaps that's why so many who have reached the top of the pyramid have fallen off. It's slippery territory. Fascinating, isn't it, that so many men and women are trying so desperately to get there?

6. Success is status.

When you add up an increase in power, privilege, and wealth, it's a simple equation. Power + privilege + wealth = status.

Last night, just before dinner, I went downstairs to take a break from the Macintosh. I took a minute to turn on CNN. The word was just coming in that the United States had attacked Iraq. I didn't do anymore writing last evening.

Instead I spent the evening switching channels between CNN, ABC, NBC, and CBS. I spent a lot of time with Dan, Peter, and Tom. Putting the war aside for a minute, I started thinking about these three men who were center stage before the entire nation during the opening hours of this war.

If anyone has "made it," they have. They have power. They have privilege. They have wealth. That all adds up to status. They have arrived. All three of them are at the top of the pyramid.

Earlier this year I was stuck in an airport so I picked up a book titled *Anchors: Brokaw, Jennings, Rather and the Evening News.* I found this revealing paragraph toward the end of the book:

> Dan Rather has been saying that he will step down as anchor when his contract runs out in 1994. Some at CBS say they wouldn't be surprised if it happens sooner than that. They say he is wearying of his job, after a decade in the anchor role. In many ways, Rather is at the peak of his personal and professional life, at about $4 million a year, the highest paid newsman ever, with a loving wife, Jean, and two grown kids, Robin and Dan, Jr. But there is one question that puzzles even Rather's admirers, and probably the anchor himself.

"The real enigma," says one CBS producer who counts himself among Rather's friends, "is why Dan hasn't enjoyed himself more. He does great stories. He has a great salary, fame, and power. He's at the top of his profession. If all that doesn't make him happy, what will?"[12]

That's the problem with cultural success. It never comes through on its promises. We latch onto it like a pilot of an F-15 locking onto an enemy fighter; yet when we make the kill, it's not quite what we thought it would be.

Cultural success promises happiness. And we believe it. We believe it so much that we pursue it wholeheartedly. We believe it so much that we begin to forget what's really important. We believe it so much that we consistently miss birthdays, anniversaries, graduations and Sunday worship. We believe it so much that we dupe ourselves into working unnecessary and ungodly hours. We believe it so much that we think we don't need a day off, although God Himself ordained that everybody should have one.

Why would people make all of those sacrifices for the sake of career advancement? They do it because they think that one day in the future, all those sacrifices will pay off. They do it because they believe that one day they can cash in their tickets on a horse named Happiness. They think that one day somewhere in the future, they will arrive. And they think that it will not only make them happy, but that it will give them a sense of significance.

According to *Anchors*, Rather has quite an office.

> His office is unquestionably the executive suite. One floor above the newsroom, he can look down on the producers below like Caesar contemplating the gladiators. It's a two-part layout, an outer and inner sanctum, and before you get to either you have to pass not one but two secretaries out front. This suite used to belong to the president of CBS News. Today, Rather resides there. As polished and decorated as an elegant stage set, the outer office includes a freshwater fish tank, an ornate, old-fashioned wood bureau, with an old manual typewriter on one side, and a computer on the other. Inside, a large Bible lies open on a book stand.[13]

If Dan would walk over to his Bible and turn the pages to James 3:13-16, he would find a scoop that would cause any news reporter to salivate. For in this passage we discover the fuel which energizes and motivates millions of people to sacrifice the most sacred and important things of life in order to get to the top of the pyramid.

In this passage, we discover the deadly pesticide of selfish ambition that poisons so many, driving them to recklessly pursue the other toxin of cultural success.

> Who among you is wise and understanding? Let him show by his good behavior his deeds in the gentleness of wisdom. But if you have bitter jealousy and *selfish ambition* in your heart, do not be

arrogant and so lie against the truth. This wisdom is not that which comes down from above, but is earthly, natural, demonic. For where jealousy and *selfish ambition* exist, there is disorder and every evil thing, (NASB, italics mine).

KILLER AMBITION

Just as there are two kinds of success: *credible* success and *cultural* success; so there are two kinds of ambition: *suitable* ambition and *selfish* ambition. James is going to clue us in on selfish ambition.

Selfish ambition is a poison. It is colorless, odorless, and tasteless. It can only be identified through the telling marks described in Scripture. James tells us three things about selfish ambition.

1. Selfish ambition is a deficient wisdom.

It is interesting that James says selfish ambition is a kind of wisdom. There are two kinds of wisdom. One is good and the other is evil. Selfish ambition is deficient when compared to the godly wisdom described in verse 17.

But the wisdom from above is first pure, then peaceable, gentle, reasonable, full of mercy and good fruits, unwavering, without hypocrisy.

We can find out more about selfish ambition simply by contrasting its traits with those of godly wisdom. Selfish ambition is the opposite of godly wisdom.

Godly Wisdom	Selfish Ambition
Pure	Impure
Peaceable	Combative
Gentle	Harsh
Reasonable (willing to yield)	Unreasonable (unwilling to yield)
Full of mercy	Without mercy
Full of good fruits	Without good fruits
Unwavering (not double-minded)	Double-minded
Without hypocrisy	Hypocritical

Two men were discussing the character of a third. "Let me describe him this way," said one to the other. "He's the kind of guy who follows you into a revolving door and comes out ahead of you." That's selfish ambition.

When I look at the list of characteristics under selfish ambition, one word comes to mind. It is the word *ruthless*. Some people are so driven to make it to the top that they will do anything to achieve their quest. They will stop at nothing to get by you. They can be combative, unreasonable, hypocritical or harsh. They are willing to do whatever it takes to get someone out of their way. They are ruthless, like Saddam Hussein. Every profession has its Saddam Husseins.

Saddam can be an attorney, a sales manager, an executive vice president of marketing, a deacon or elder on a church board, or an insecure pastor trying to climb the denominational ladder. Wherever you find these Saddams, they have one thing in common. They are ruthless—and it is selfish ambition that drives them. That's why their lives are so pathetic and deficient.

2. Selfish ambition is an inferior wisdom.

Why is it inferior? It is inferior because it is earthly. It is inferior because it does not come down from heaven. It is also described as natural. Once again, that makes it inferior, because the wisdom that God offers us is supernatural. So selfish ambition is inferior and natural. It is also very popular.

> Everyone knew Malcolm Stevenson Forbes. He was the rich macho magazine publisher with a big, loving family, a perpetual ear-to-ear smile and glinty eyes behind black-rimmed glasses. Elizabeth Taylor was his girlfriend, and virtually every chairman of every major company on the planet was his buddy. . . . His multi-million-dollar parties were envied because he and his guests had such unbridled fun reinforcing the image of a man spending money as fast as he could.
> But away from the paparazzi, the big-top extravaganzas, the celebrities, behind the broad smile resided a different Malcolm. The urbane charm and the wit faded a little. Instead there was a hint of discontent in this luckiest of men who was envied for having everything.[14]

Christopher Winans, in his book, *Malcolm Forbes: The Man Who Had Everything*, tells of a motorcycle tour that Forbes took through Egypt in 1984 with his Capitalist Tool motorcycle team.

After viewing the staggering burial tomb of King Tut, Forbes seemed to be in a reflective mood.

As they were returning to the hotel in a shuttle bus, Forbes turned to one of his associates and asked with all sincerity: "Do you think I'll be remembered after I die?"

Forbes *is* remembered. He is remembered as the man who coined the phrase, "He who dies with the most toys wins." That was the wisdom of Malcolm Forbes. In fact, that was his ambition. That's why he collected scores of motorcycles. That's why he would pay over a million dollars for a Fabergé egg. That's why he owned castles, hot air balloons and countless other toys that he can no longer access.

The Lord Jesus Christ gave us words of superior wisdom when he said, "What good will it be for a man if he gains the whole world, yet forfeits his soul?" (Matthew 16:26). It is a fatally deficient wisdom that declares "He who dies with the most toys wins."

Few people in history have great monuments like King Tut. Few people will have a memorial service like the one held for Malcolm Forbes. Dignitaries from all over the world attended his funeral.

But we will all be remembered. It was Cato the Elder who once remarked, "I would rather have men ask, after I am dead, why I have no monument than why I have one." In the final analysis, there is only one thing that people remember, and it isn't how much we had in our toy chests. It is our character.

C. H. Spurgeon poignantly stated it this way: "A good character is the best tombstone. Those who loved you, and were helped by you, will remember you. So carve your name on hearts, and not on marble."

That is wisdom from above. And you don't get it with selfish ambition. What have you been carving on lately?

3. Selfish ambition is the very wisdom of Satan.

James tells us that selfish ambition is demonic. The demons are fallen angels who chose to join the rebellion of Satan, emulating his example in insanely defying the eternal plan of God. People who indulge their selfish ambition are being gripped by the same powerful spirit that deluded angelic beings into revolting against the Father, the Son, and the Holy Spirit.

Selfish ambition first occurred in the heart of Satan in ages past. As we read Isaiah 14:12-14, we get a glimpse into the magnitude of the selfish ambition of the highest ranking angel of the angelic order.

How you have fallen from heaven, O star of the morning,
    son of the dawn!
You have been cut down to the earth, you who have weakened the
    nations!
But you said in your heart,
        "*I will* ascend to heaven;
            I will raise my throne above the stars of God,
            And *I will* sit on the mount of assembly in the
                recesses of the north.
            I will ascend above the heights of the clouds;
            I will make myself like the Most High" (NASB, italics
                mine).

Satan was already at the top of the angelic ladder according to Ezekiel 28:12-19. He was at the apex. He had it all. He had power and he had position. But it wasn't enough, for he realized there was One greater than he. That was something he couldn't live with. Notice that he uttered five "I wills." And notice that he didn't utter them verbally. He thought them in his heart.

He not only wanted to become like God, he wanted to raise his throne above the throne of God. That was the bottom line of his selfish ambition. In other words, *he desired for God to worship him*. Satan desired nothing less than to become the ultimate Number One. He refused to be satisfied with who he was and with what he had been given. His craving to be #1 devoured him. And that same Satanic craving is luring countless others.

Back in the sixties, a group known as the Nylons had a big hit. It went like this:

In the jungle, the mighty jungle,
the lion sleeps tonight.
In the jungle, the quiet jungle,

the lion sleeps tonight.
In the village, the peaceful village,
the lion sleeps tonight.
In the village, the quiet village,
the lion sleeps tonight.

We live in a jungle, too. Only our jungles have freeways, cellular phones, and fax machines to enable us to keep up the frantic pace required of those who would be culturally successful. But one thing should be noted. Our jungle does have a lion, and he is very real and dangerous. "Be of sober spirit, be on the alert. Your adversary, the devil, prowls about like a roaring lion, seeking someone to devour" (1 Peter 5:8, NASB).

This lion not only roars, he devours. He devours people and he devours their relationships.

In the jungle, the fast track jungle,
the lion roars tonight.
In the jungle, the competitive jungle,
the lion roars tonight.
In the suburbs, the affluent suburbs,
the lion devours tonight.
In the suburbs, the stressed-out suburbs,
the lion devours tonight.

It should be noted that Satan does not work alone. He is not the only lion in the jungle. A group of demonic entities follows his leadership. They too are lions. Not as strong, not as cunning, but lions nonetheless. It has been observed that lions rarely hunt alone. They usually hunt in groups. Do you know what a group of lions on the hunt is called? It is called a pride.

I find that of interest because wherever you find the influence of Satan and his fellow demonic lions, you will always find pride. Pride is the root sin that caused Satan to fall. Pride is, in fact, the flip side of selfish ambition. When selfish ambition and pride fuel my life, I am acting out in my own experience the demonic insanity role-modeled by Satan. The result is appallingly destructive. James tells us that where selfish ambition exists there is disorder and every evil thing.

We could say the same thing of pride. C.S. Lewis made some priceless observations about pride. Let's listen to him:

> According to Christian teachers, the essential vice, the utmost evil, is Pride. Unchastity, anger, greed, drunkenness, and all that, are mere fleabites in comparison: it was through Pride that the devil became the devil: Pride leads to every other vice: it is the complete anti-God state of mind.

> Does this seem to you exaggerated? If so, think it over. I pointed out a moment ago that the more pride one had, the more one disliked pride in others. In fact, if you want to find out how proud you are the easiest way is to ask yourself, "How much do I dislike it when other people snub me, or refuse to take any notice of me? . . ."

> The point is that each person's pride is in competition with everyone else's pride. It is because I wanted to be the big noise at the party that I am so annoyed at someone else being the big noise. . . . Now what you want to get clear is that Pride is essentially competitive, is competitive by its very nature, while the other vices are competitive only, so to speak, by accident.

> Pride gets no pleasure out of having something, only out of having more of it than the next man. We say that people are proud of being richer, or cleverer, or better looking than others. If every one else became equally rich, or clever, or good looking there would be nothing to be proud about. It is the comparison that makes you proud: the pleasure of being above the rest.[15]

Let me ask you a question. Why do you want to climb your ladder? It may be the corporate ladder, the academic ladder, the military ladder, the political ladder, or the ministry ladder. But the question is, why? Is it legitimately to provide for your family and to use your skills to make a contribution, or is it simply to try and rise above the pack?

Every single one of us deals with pride. I can tell you it is as rampant among those of us in full-time ministry as it is in your profession. It was rampant in Paul's day for he said that some "proclaim Christ out of selfish ambition, rather than from pure motives" (Philippians 1:17). None of us are exempt from pride, as none of us are exempt from selfish ambition.

Benjamin Franklin once said that "there is perhaps not one of our natural passions so hard to subdue as pride. Beat it down, stifle it, mortify it as much as one pleases, it is still alive. Even if I could conceive that I had completely overcome it, I should probably be proud of my humility."

Of course, there is a good kind of pride. We could call it decent pride; it is what we feel when we do something with all of our heart without trying to outdo someone else. Decent pride comes from doing a splendid job of refinishing that old antique bookcase that was in the garage for so long. Decent pride comes from working hard in third grade to learn your multiplication tables. Decent pride comes from putting in a hard day's work simply because it is the right thing to do. Decent pride is a person working to do their best without any thought of topping someone else. Decent pride is not related to deadly pride. It is, however, a first cousin of credible success.

Destructive pride is the killer. It is the Killer of killers, and Poison of poisons. Lewis is right: "Pride is spiritual cancer: it eats up the very possibility of love, or contentment, or even common sense." Pride and selfish ambition are the reasons why untold millions are sacrificing their marriages, their families, their integrity, and their reputations in order to do whatever it takes to further their careers.

In his aptly titled autobiography, *The Price of Success*, J. B. Phillips tells of the destructive power of success in his own life. "Phillips began translating the New Testament Epistles to encourage his bomb-threatened London congregation. From this humble beginning, and with C.S. Lewis's enthusiastic support, a dynamic and prodigious writing career was launched. Radio broadcasting established his reputation as a natural communicator and requests for him to lecture snowballed. . . ." This is how Phillips reacted:

I was in a state of excitement throughout the whole of 1955. My work hardly seemed arduous for it was intrinsically exciting. I was tasting the sweets of success to an almost unimaginable degree. My health was excellent; my future prospects were rosier than my wildest dreams could ever suggest; applause, honor and appreciation met me wherever I went. . . . I was not aware of the dangers of success. The subtle corrosion of character, the unconscious changing of values, and the secret monstrous growth of a vastly inflated idea of myself seeped slowly into me. Vaguely, I was aware of this, and like some frightful parody of St. Augustine, I prayed, "Lord, make me humble, *but not yet.*"[16]

The pursuit of success nearly ruined Phillips. It was so subtle he didn't realize what it was doing to him. An old African proverb exudes wisdom: "It's on the path you do not fear that the wild beast catches you." Phillips didn't realize that he should have a healthy fear of success, and it nearly ate him alive.

May I be perfectly candid? It is precisely at this point that we are in great danger. If you have been reading along and think that this discussion is very interesting but that it really doesn't relate to you, then it very much relates to you. The enemy would have us believe that this is something other people need to hear about—but not us. That is selfish ambition in action. Phillips did not realize what was happening to him; neither have countless others. We are up against a very sly adversary. He would like nothing better than to dupe you into thinking you are on secure ground when it comes to this area of your life.

That's why selfish ambition is the very wisdom of Satan. If it is the wisdom of Satan, wouldn't you expect it to be subtle and hard to detect? It, too, is colorless, odorless, and tasteless. Fortunately, there is an antidote.

C. S. Lewis closed his comments on pride with these words:

> If anyone would like to acquire humility, I can, I think, tell him the first step. The first step is to realize that one is proud. And a biggish step, too. At least, nothing whatever can be done before it. If you think you are not conceited, you are very conceited indeed.[17]

My friend, if you have been eaten up with pride and selfish ambition, then join the club. We are all poisoned by it. We must detox ourselves every day. The good news is that we can be set free by the power of the Holy Spirit. Admit your pride to Him. Admit your selfish ambition. And hand it to Christ. That is the antidote. A. W. Tozer said it well years ago:

> In this world men are judged by their ability to do. The effort to succeed puts too much strain on the nerves. Excessive preoccupation with the struggle to win narrows the mind, hardens the heart, and shuts out a thousand bright visions which might be enjoyed if there were only leisure to notice them. The mania to succeed is a good thing perverted. The desire to fulfill the purpose for which we were created is of course a gift from God, but sin has twisted this impulse about and turned it into a selfish lust for first place and top honors. By this lust the whole world is driven by a demon

. . . When we come to Christ we enter a different world.[18]

Christ has called us to live in this jungle for Him. We are to be in the jungle, but not of the jungle. He is looking for men and women who can function in the jungle by depending, not on the world's wisdom, but on His. That's what this book is all about. It's not about leaving the jungle, it's about overcoming in the jungle. It's about functioning in the jungle according to the wisdom of the ultimate Lion, the Lion of Judah.

Tarzan traveled through the jungle by clinging onto and swinging from vines. We are to do exactly the same thing. There is only one way to travel through the jungle in a way that will provide safety and security from the threats of the jungle. If you desire to live in the jungle with balance, grace, and skill, then, like Tarzan, grab a vine. If you desire to have a godly home in a godless generation, then, like Tarzan, grab a vine. If you desire to have a home characterized by spiritual depth instead of materialistic superficiality, then, like Tarzan, grab a vine. But you can't just grab any vine—and I say this not flippantly, but with great reverence—you must lay hold of *the* Vine, the One who said, "I am the Vine. . . ." That is, grab hold of the Lord Jesus Christ *and don't let go.*

Now, Jesus was talking about a different kind of vine. The metaphor is different but the principle is the same. "I am the vine, and you are the branches. Apart from me you can do nothing." That's the secret to getting through the jungle.

There is only one way to survive in our modern cultural jungle and it's by living in complete dependence upon Jesus. What have you been holding onto lately? Whatever it is, may the Lord give you the wisdom to let go of it and lay hold of Him. The answer to making it in the jungle has never been alcohol or any other chemical substance. It is clinging to the Vine. For apart from Him, you can do nothing.

Notes

1. Douglas LaBier, *Modern Madness* (Menlo Park, CA: Addison Wesley, 1986), 51

2. *Wall Street Journal,* November 6, 1990, B6

3. Cited by Dr. Dean Ornish, *Reversing Heart Disease* (New York:

Random House, 1990), 77

4. Terry Hershey, *Young Adult Ministry* (Loveland, CO: Group Books, 1986), 39

5. Ibid., 39.

6. Anthony Campolo, cited by John Johnston, *Christian Excellence* (Grand Rapids: Baker), 1985.

7. George J. Marlin, editor, *The Quotable Chesterton* (San Francisco: Ignatius Press, 1986), 333

8. John Johnston, *Christian Excellence*, 30.

9. *American Heritage*, "The Business of America," Peter Baida, November, 1987.

10. Nightingale Conant Direct Mail Advertisement.

11. Donald Trump, *The Art of the Deal* (New York: Random House, 1987), dust jacket.

12. Robert Goldberg, *Anchors: Brokaw, Jennings, Rather and the Evening News* (New York: Birch Lane Press), 1990.

13. Ibid.

14. Christopher Winans, *Malcolm Forbes: The Man Who Had Everything* (New York: St. Martin's Press), 1990.

15. C. S. Lewis, *The Best of C.S. Lewis* (Washington D.C.: Christianity Today, Inc., 1969), 497.

16. J. B. Phillips, *The Price of Success* (Wheaton, Ill.: Harold Shaw Publishers, 1984).

17. C. S. Lewis, *The Best*, 497.

18. A. W. Tozer, source unknown.

Chapter 3

CHILD SACRIFICE

Jesus loves the little children,
all the children of the world.
                              A child's hymn

I don't think you are going to like this chapter. I certainly didn't enjoy writing it. I asked several friends to read it before it went to the publisher and they didn't like it either. Then I gave it to the publisher and no one there liked it. But interestingly enough, they all agreed it should be in the book.

This is a chapter about child sacrifice. I'll warn you in advance that it is strong stuff. These days if a book is going to be well-received, it better be compelling, exciting, and enticing. I have found it very difficult to make the subject of child sacrifice exciting and enticing. But it is compelling.

Several of my friends thought they knew where I was going with this chapter. In the back of their minds they thought this must be about abortion. They were wrong. The direction of this chapter will probably surprise you. That's why my friends who didn't like this chapter thought that it should be included.

Now perhaps you may be wondering, *what in the world does child sacrifice have to do with better homes and jungles?*

The answer is this: children have always been sacrificed in the jungle. How many times have you heard someone use the phrase "It's a jungle out there"? That is a very profound statement. And it is true.

Our jungles may look different from those in the Amazon or in

Africa, but they are jungles nonetheless. And children are being sacrificed everyday in the "civilized" jungles of America. They are being sacrificed in my neighborhood and in yours. Child sacrifice is not a pleasant subject. But trust me—it is a necessary one.

THE BIG PICTURE

Child sacrifice has occurred throughout history. Even in the supposedly civilized twentieth century, the sacrifice of children has been a fairly regular practice.

Hitler made it an everyday activity in the concentration camps of Germany. The Supreme Court made it legal in America in 1973 with its *Roe vs. Wade* decision. As a result, America is plagued with cash-motivated abortion clinics that litter the landscape of every town, city, and village.

Sacrificing children is nothing unique to this century. History gives ample evidence of the popularity of killing infants from the earliest days of human civilization. Will Durant, in *Our Oriental Heritage*, documents how widespread the practice of child sacrifice had become in various tribes across the world. Many of these tribes resided in jungles:

> Most nature peoples permitted the killing of the newborn child if it was deformed, or diseased, or a bastard, or if its mother died in giving it birth. . . . Many tribes killed infants whom they considered to have been born under unlucky circumstances: so the Bondei natives strangled all children who entered the world headfirst; the Kamchadals killed babies born in stormy weather; Madagascar tribes exposed, drowned, or buried alive children who made their debut in March or April, or on a Wednesday or a Friday, or in the last week of the month.
>
> If a woman gave birth to twins, it was, in some tribes, held proof of adultery, since no man could be the father of two children at the same time; and therefore one or both of the children suffered death. The practice of infanticide was particularly prevalent among nomads, who found children a problem on their long marches.
>
> The Bangerang tribe of Victoria killed half their children at birth; the Lenguas of the Paraguayan Chaco allowed only one child per family per seven years to survive; the Abipones achieved a French economy in population by rearing a boy and a girl in each household, killing off other offspring as they appeared.
>
> Where famine conditions existed or threatened, most tribes strangled

the newborn, and some tribes ate them. Usually it was the girl that was most subject to infanticide, occasionally she was tortured to death with a view to inducing the soul to appear, in the next incarnation, in the form of a boy.[1]

But child sacrifice is not restricted to primitive tribes living in jungles. When the children of Israel were ordered to take over Canaan, they were instructed to utterly destroy the inhabitants. God had seen the perversity of the Canaanites. They regularly practiced every kind of sexual indecency. As a result, the entire culture, including thousands upon thousands of children, were shot through with venereal disease. The Canaanites also regularly sacrificed children as part of their myth and ritual. God commanded their destruction so that such practices would not influence Israel. But Israel did not eradicate the morally cancerous Canaanites, and it was just a matter of time before the cancer spread through the people of God.

Manasseh was the son of King Hezekiah. The scriptures make it clear that his personal evil was so great that he surpassed the wickedness of the Canaanites. Manasseh became so twisted in his thinking that he sacrificed his firstborn son to the god Molech. Think of it! Child sacrifice actually became a reality among God's people.

Francis Schaeffer, the late twentieth century prophet, described the ritual of child sacrifice in his book, *The Church Before the Watching World*:

> Molech, whose idol was in the valley Hinnom, was a heathen god whom the Jews were constantly warned against following. What kind of god was Molech? He was the god of the sacrifice of newborn babies. This was the central act of his worship; the firstborn of every woman's body had to be sacrificed to Molech. According to one tradition, there was an opening at the back of the brazen idol, and after a fire was made within it, each parent had to come and with his own hands place his firstborn child in the white-hot, outstretched hands of Molech. According to the tradition, the parent was not allowed to show emotion, and drums were beaten so that the baby's cries could not be heard as the baby died in the hands of Molech.[2]

As one turns the pages of the Bible and history, child sacrifice turns up time and time again. In the book of Exodus, Pharaoh ordered the Hebrew midwives to kill all newborn Hebrew males. Centuries later, the Gospels record that Herod, in an attempt to snuff out the life of the King of kings, ordered the slaughter of all Hebrew baby boys in Bethlehem. In both situations, God stepped in and protected two infants who would alter the course of history. Interesting, isn't it, that two separate kings, living hundreds of years apart, attempted to kill both Moses and the infant Christ?

As we have seen, child sacrifice is often associated with religion. Both the Aztecs and the Incas were very religious people. And both civilizations practiced child sacrifice in staggering proportions:

> . . . Whenever an Inca emperor died, the toll was terrible. Hundreds of maidens would be drugged, beheaded, and buried with the dead ruler. Hundreds of others would die whenever the state faced a difficult problem or decision. Stolid priests proclaimed that only thus would the gods be pleased to help, and so the beautiful boys and girls died on the reeking altars . . .

Among the Aztec, the toll of sacrifice stuns the mind.

> In the last years before the Spanish conquest, a thousand of the finest children and young people were offered up *each week*. Dressed in splendid robes, they were drugged and then helped up the steps of the highpyramids and held down upon the altars. A priest, bloody knife in hand, parted the robes, made a quick incision, reached in his other hand and drew forth the heart, still beating, which he held high before the people assembled in the plaza below. . . . A thousand a week of the finest among the children and youth, who huddled in prison before their turns came. It is no wonder that all of the enemies of the Aztec rushed to become allies of the conquering Spaniards and helped to overthrow that brutal regime.[3]

The Middle Ages, the period of the Crusades in the Holy Land, was no stranger to child sacrifice. Tremendous wars were waged in Palestine which spilled oceans of blood for nearly five hundred years.

In 1212 a French shepherd boy by the name of Steven claimed that Jesus had appeared to him disguised as a pilgrim. Supposedly, Jesus instructed him to take a letter to the king of France. This poor, misguided boy told everyone he saw about what he thought he had encountered. Before long he had gathered a large following of more than thirty thousand children who accompanied him on his pilgrimage. As Philip Schaff records it, when asked where they were going, they replied, "We go to God, and seek for the holy cross beyond the sea." They reached Marseilles, but the waves did not part and let them go through dry-shod as they expected.[4]

It was at Marseilles that tragedy occurred. The children met two men, Hugo Ferreus and William Porcus. The men claimed to be so impressed with the calling of the children that they offered to transport them across the Mediterranean in seven ships without charge. What the children didn't know was that the two men were slave traders. The children boarded the ships and the journey began, but instead of setting sail for the Holy Land they set course for North Africa, "where they were sold as slaves in the Muslim markets that did a large business in the buying and selling of human beings. Few if any returned. None ever reached the Holy Land."[5] Two cunning men enjoyed enormous financial profits simply because they were willing to sacrifice the lives of thousands of children.

Schaff writes that as "impossible as such a movement might seem to our calculating age, it is attested by too many good witnesses to permit its being relegated to the realm of legend, and the trials and death of the children of the thirteenth century will continue to be associated with the slaughter of the children of Bethlehem at the hand of Herod."[6]

It seems hard to comprehend, but throughout history, adults have been willing to sacrifice children when it seemed necessary or profitable to do so.

THE EPIDEMIC FORECAST

Children are not only susceptible to sacrifice, but like their parents, they are subject to epidemics. The notion of an epidemic is foreign to most baby boomers, living as they do in the comfort and health of American society. We give thought from time to time to the possibilities of earthquakes, tornadoes, and hurricanes, but the threat of an epidemic hardly crosses our minds. When we were young, before Jonas Salk developed his vaccine, our parents worried that one of their children might succumb to polio. But the most serious epidemic that most of us baby boomers have ever faced is a breakout of influenza in the local schools.

Does such an outbreak strike fear in our hearts? Hardly. If our child isn't feeling well and has a slight temperature, we chalk it up to the "flu." We know he will be fine in a day or two. This was not always the case. For centuries, influenza was feared as a killer of children.

> Epidemics of influenza commonly affect a high percentage of the population . . . the frequency of illness is greatest in children, although the impression widely prevails that adults are most commonly attacked. . . .
>
> The 1918 epidemic was the most destructive in history; in fact it ranks with the plague of Justinian and the Black Death as one of the severest holocausts of disease ever encountered. It was estimated . . . that more than 20,000,000 persons perished of influenza in a few months and more than 50 times as many were sick. In the United States 548,000 died. In India, 12,500,000 persons or 4 percent of the total population, are said to have been killed by influenza in the autumn of 1918.[7]

Children and parents alike succumbed to the epidemic of influenza. Can you imagine 20 million people dying from the flu? As incredible as that seems, another epidemic was even more devastating. I'm referring to the Black Death. Between 1347 and 1370, nearly 40 million died from the plague. Estimates vary, but educated guesses place the death toll somewhere between one-third and one-half of the entire population of Europe.

Precisely what was the Black Death? Plague is primarily a disease of rodents, usually rats. It is carried from one rat to another by the rat flea, but human beings can catch the disease if they become infested with fleas. In the crowded conditions of medieval cities, whole populations commonly did just that. In times of extreme stress, during sieges or famines, city dwellers were especially at risk. If plague became epidemic, as often happened, the death toll was terrible, for there was no known cure. (Only modern antibiotics can control the disease.)

A MODERN EPIDEMIC

I don't know any families that have lost a child to influenza. I don't know of any families in our neighborhood desperately trying to fight off the plague. We are fortunate to live in an age in which medical technology has immunized us against many of the killers that have wiped out entire families in the past.

But there is another epidemic taking a tremendous toll on our children. It is not influenza and it is not the plague. The epidemic wiping out families all across America is affluenza. It doesn't come from rats. It comes from the rat race.

> Now I lay me down to sleep
> I pray my Cuisinart to keep
> I pray my stocks are on the rise
> And that my analyst is wise
> That all the wine I sip is white
> And that my hot tub's watertight
> That racquetball won't get too tough
> That all my sushi's fresh enough
> I pray my cordless phone still works
> That my career won't lose it perks
> My microwave won't radiate
> My condo won't depreciate
> I pray my health club doesn't close
> And that my money market grows
> If I go broke before I wake
> I pray my Volvo they won't take[8]

Affluenza is not found only in wealthy families. Affluenza is becoming epidemic in the "lives of those who are merely well off, who are comfortable middle-class, or who simply aspire to greater incomes, acquisitions, and status."[9] In other words, the majority of families in America are at risk when it comes to affluenza.

Affluenza attacks relationships. Family relationships. The ones who inevitably suffer most are our children. Affluenza causes parents to sacrifice their children on the altar of success. Affluenza is a subtle killer. It first attacks the parents, who pass it on to their children.

Affluenza is a spiritual virus that moves slowly enough to keep people from realizing they have been infected. But it does have a number of distinguishing marks. Affluenza is the:

- desire for more and more, despite what we already have;

- insatiable drive to be successful without ever experiencing contentment;
  - practice of consistently choosing career over family;
  - unchecked yearning for more possessions and wealth;
  - unwillingness to settle for less than the best of everything.

PRESSURE COOKER FAMILIES

A family afflicted with affluenza is characterized by intense pressure. There is tremendous pressure to succeed, to keep up, to stay on top, to be number one, to excel in career, athletics, and school. As a result, there is little time for quietness, solitude, and personal reflection. Everyone is too busy trying to make it to the top.

- Affluenza causes parents to give their children too much freedom and too little attention.
- Affluenza causes parents to give their kids too many things and too little time.
- Affluenza causes parents to pressure their children to perform instead of encouraging them to develop at a natural pace.
- Affluenza causes parents to give their children too much information which erodes their moral innocence.
- Affluenza causes parents to be focused on acquiring an image rather than on achieving character.

Affluenza always begins with the parents. Children catch it from their mom and dad. That's how the epidemic gets started. Now, it is possible for children to catch it from other children who have been infected by their parents. But the antidote to having your kids catch it from another family is for you (the parent) to just say no.

The awful thing about affluenza is that it hits parents who really do love their children. It is so insidious. Affluenza severely affects our ability to discern. It begins to cloud our judgment and eventually begins to distort our value system. Affluenza brings about a slow change in the way we think about what is important in life. Before you know it—if you take a deep look inside—you will find that affluenza causes you to value things over people. Those people will probably be your spouse and children. They are the ones who always suffer most from cases of affluenza.

Affluenza prompts us to do things we would never do if we were seeing clearly. That is precisely what is so sinister about it; it clouds and distorts our judgment. Before you know it, affluenza begins to affect your behavior.

• Affluenza can make you uncivilized.

• Affluenza can make you behave as though you really did live in a jungle.

• Affluenza ultimately will cause you to sacrifice your children.

When affluenza has you in its grip, you will spout all kinds of wonderful explanations to explain away your behavior. That's another symptom I failed to mention about affluenza. It always comes with a full set of rationalizations.

JUNGLE CHEERLEADING

Channelview, Texas, is a neat, middle-class suburb of Houston. It's a typical bedroom community of nice homes, nice cars, and plenty of carpools. The competition is fierce in athletics, all the way up from first grade to high school. Recently the competition got a little ugly. But not in football or basketball. In cheerleading.

Amber Heath and Shanna Harper live right around the corner from each other. They have been friends for years. Amber is president of the student council and Shanna is vice-president. For years not only have the two girls been friends, but their mothers have been as well. The girls both went to the same private Christian school and the moms would take turns driving the kids to school. Everything was fine between the two families . . . until sixth grade. That's when Amber beat out Shanna for cheerleader.

According to a local pastor, the two girls had always competed against each other. But Amber had been competing in beauty and talent contests since she was four, and she always seemed to get the edge over Shanna. Shanna's mom, who attends a local evangelical church several times a week (she's the church organist), apparently began to resent the pattern of her daughter consistently losing out to Amber. So she took matters into her own hands.

Two years ago she tried unsuccessfully to get Amber disqualified from the cheerleading competition by invoking a technicality in the rules. Last year she showed up at school the day students were voting for cheerleader candidates and handed out rulers and pencils bearing the slogan "Shanna Harper Cheerleader." But as a result of her mother's action, Shanna was disqualified.[10]

This church organist apparently could take it no longer. So she allegedly tried to hire a hit man to kill both Amber and her mother. She wasn't sure who would do such a thing, and mentioned it one day to her former brother-in-law. He notified the police, who wired an officer who posed as the hit man. According to the tape recording, the "hit man" told her the price would be $5,000 for killing the mother and $2,500 for killing the daughter. Mrs. Holloway couldn't come up with that much money in cash. So she gave the "hit man" a pair of diamond earrings as a downpayment for killing just the mother.

According to a police sergeant, "She really wanted the daughter done to get her completely out of the picture, but she figured if she got mom done that would upset the daughter enough to take her out of the picture."[11] She wanted to "cause Amber so much emotional grief that she would not be a threat to Shanna in the rigorous competition for slots on next year's freshman cheerleading squad at Channelview High School."[12]

Mrs. Holloway was arrested for solicitation of capital murder and released on $10,000 bail. She has pleaded not guilty to the charges. The entire town of Channelview is in shock. According to one insider, "She was living her life through Shanna. Shanna's achievements were all she had, and it had become an obsession."[13]

According to Lieutenant Charles Shaffer of the Harris County Organized Crime Task Force, almost all murders for hire fall into one of two categories. "It's usually either money or love when someone goes out and solicits a murder. This case has its bizarre twists, but it basically fits the pattern. The motive here was love, a mother's love for her daughter."[14]

According to one report, some neighbors in the Sterling Green subdivision where the two families live wondered whether the incident had lessons for every parent who has supported a child in competition. "We all go through that," said Chris Netherly, thirty-one. "We try to give our kids things we didn't have."[15]

That last statement is profound. For the root cause of this bizarre behavior was nothing more than affluenza trying to give a child something a parent didn't have. It may be a toy, it may be a car, it may be popularity, it may be fame, it may be status in the community.

Do you see from this tragic example how affluenza can cause someone from an evangelical, Bible-teaching church to act in an uncivilized manner? Do you see how affluenza can cloud and distort our judgment? Do you see how affluenza can begin to affect our behavior? The fact is this: affluenza really can make us behave as though we live in a jungle. Affluenza really can make us uncivilized. And ultimately, affluenza caused this woman to sacrifice her child.

She obviously didn't do what Manasseh or the Aztecs did. She didn't try to kill her own child. But allegedly she was willing to kill someone else's child. When that was too expensive, she was willing to kill the parent. But when you get right down to it, she did sacrifice her own child. She sacrificed her daughter's entire life. For Shanna will never be the same again because of a mother who was willing to go to any lengths to ensure that her daughter was "successful." Living in the jungle made this woman uncivilized—uncivilized enough to sacrifice her daughter's reputation, her daughter's name, and her daughter's future. Will her daughter ever be able to put this behind her? I'll let you answer that.

The apostle John once wrote these living words:

> Love not the jungle, nor the things in the jungle. If anyone loves the jungle, the love of the Father is not in him.
> For all that is in the jungle, the lust of the flesh and the lust of the eyes and the boastful pride of life, is not from the Father, but is from the jungle (1 John 2:15-16).

Now, you and I both know that John did not use the term "jungle." Rather, he used the term "world." But perhaps "jungle" is not a poor synonym for what goes on in our world. "World," in the original language, has the idea of a world system. According to Rienecker and Rogers, two Greek scholars, it can "signify mankind organized in rebellion against God."[16]

That's why it's a jungle out there. We have to live in that system every day and it can begin to influence us without our knowing it. Dave Roper, in his excellent book, *The Strength of a Man*, comments on worldliness:

> The Bible defines worldliness by centering morality where we intuitively know it should be. Worldliness is the lust of the flesh (a passion for sensual satisfaction), the lust of the eyes (an inordinate desire for the finer things of life), and the pride of life (self-satisfaction in who we are, what we have, and what we have done).
>
> Worldliness, then, is a *preoccupation* with ease and affluence. It elevates creature comfort to the point of idolatry; large salaries and comfortable life-styles become necessities of life. Worldliness is reading magazines about people who live hedonistic lives and spend too much money on themselves and wanting to be like them. But more importantly, worldliness is simply pride and selfishness in disguise. It's being resentful when someone snubs us or patronizes us or shows off. It means smarting under every slight, challenging every word spoken against us, cringing when another is preferred before us. Worldliness is harboring grudges, nursing grievances, and wallowing in self-pity. These are the ways in which we are most like the world.[17]

Affluenza is worldliness in drag. It's the current American version of what the apostle John warned us about nearly two millennia ago.

Recently I went in to see my doctor and get a physical. Unfortunately, I got some bad news. My cholesterol level was over 260. It should be under 200. Not only was my cholesterol too high, but the doctor pointed out the difference between my HDL (good cholesterol) and LDL (bad cholesterol). The test showed I had way too much bad cholesterol and not nearly enough good cholesterol.

I walked into that office feeling fine. I came out feeling not so fine. Especially since I had a grandfather and an uncle who both died of heart attacks in their early fifties. They had their first heart attacks in their early forties. I am forty-one.

I thought long and hard about the situation. Then I started to do some research. I found out that if I would radically control my diet, I could significantly control my cholesterol. The problem was the fat in my diet. As I read the nutritional information, it became apparent that almost everything I liked was loaded with fat. This was going to require a major change. I thought about it all week, figuring out what I was going to do.

I was speaking that Friday evening to a group of about nine hundred people. As I was about halfway through the talk, I started getting sharp, jagged pains in my chest.

I made it through the talk with no problem. When I got back to my room I stopped thinking about a change in my diet and decided to make a change in my diet. A radical change.

Just one week prior to the jabbing chest pains I did not know I had such high cholesterol. I was living my life as though there were no problems. I would eat what I wanted without giving a lot of thought to what I was eating. I thought everything was fine . . . but it wasn't.

No, let's be honest here. I *did* know I had high cholesterol. Three years ago I went into a doctor's office for a physical and my cholesterol level was almost identical to my recent test. But for the last three years I have lived as if I didn't have high cholesterol. Oh, I made some minor adjustments in my diet. Instead of two scoops of ice cream, I'd have one. But that was about it. I was deceiving myself about what I knew to be true. I was living in a state of denial.

That's exactly the nature of sin. The *modus operandi* of sin is always deceit. Ephesians 4:22 speaks of the lusts of *deceit*. Hebrews 3:13 warns of being hardened by the *deceitfulness* of sin. Sin's method in both my life and yours is always deceit. That's why it is so easy to look at someone else who is extreme in their behavior and think we would never do such a thing. The truth is, we *could* do such a thing. Deceit tells us that we couldn't, but deceit is a liar.

As I thought it over, it became clear to me that if I did have a heart attack, I would be quick to make some radical changes in my lifestyle. I would probably follow a strict diet with great motivation! And then I thought, *well, why not go ahead and make the changes before you have a heart attack?* That's why for the last three months I've been eating like a hippie from the 1960s. And do you know what? My cholesterol level is going down. But before I could tackle my cholesterol, I had to get to work on deceit. Deceit was telling me that everything was OK when it wasn't.

Affluenza also affects my heart, my spiritual heart. It is easy to sit here and write about affluenza in someone else's life. It is easy to write about someone who would be so driven to have a successful child that she would try to negotiate a contract with a hit man. It is easy to sit here and write about Channelview and think to myself, *I would never do anything like that*. And I probably wouldn't. But the point is, I easily *could*. And so could you.

> The heart is more deceitful than all else
> And is desperately sick;
> Who can understand it? (Jeremiah 17:9, NASB)

According to Jeremiah, our hearts are not in good shape. We can easily deceive ourselves because that is the natural condition of the heart. We can deceive ourselves into thinking that we would never do what other people do. But we can. When you get down to it, we are all the same on the inside.

> The worst enemy that you have is yourself. He occupies the same skin that you occupy. He uses the same brain that you do in thinking his destructive thoughts. He uses the same hands that you use to perform his own deeds. This enemy can do you more harm than anyone else. He is the greatest handicap that you have in your daily Christian life.
>
> There are two factors that make dealing with this enemy doubly difficult. In the first place, we are reluctant to recognize and identify him. We are loath to label him as an enemy. The fact of the matter is most of us rather like him. The second problem is that he is on the inside of us. If he would only come out and fight like a man, it would be different, but he will not. It is not because he is a coward, but because he can fight better from his position within.[18]

My greatest problem is me; your greatest problem is you. Call it sin, call it worldliness, call it affluenza, but our greatest problem lies within us.

> Alexander the Great was probably the greatest military genius who has moved armies across the pages of history. There has been no one like him. Before the age of thirty-five he had conquered the world, but he died a drunkard. He had conquered the world, but he could not conquer Alexander the Great.[19]

Over one hundred years ago, Bishop J. C. Ryle wrote about the awful power of sin:

> I am convinced that the greatest proof of the extent and power of sin is the pertinacity with which it cleaves to man even after he is converted and has become the subject of the Holy Ghost's operations. . . . This infection of nature doth remain, even in them that are regenerate. So deeply planted are the roots of human corruption, that even after we are born again, renewed, "washed, sanctified, justified," and made living members of Christ, these roots remain alive in the bottom of our hearts, and, like the leprosy in the walls of the house, we never get rid of them until the earthly house of this tabernacle is dissolved.[20]

When we come to Christ, the *dominion* of sin in our lives is broken. But we are kidding ourselves if we think it is just going to fade away. It will not.

There's something else about the deceit of affluenza that I cannot fail to mention. Satan is described by the Lord Jesus Christ as the "father of liars." He is not just a liar, he is a subtle liar. Affluenza lies to us. The subtle deceit of affluenza is that it promises something to us that it will never deliver. What does it promise? It promises satisfaction. That's why it is so compelling.

We think that if we just get that promotion, or are invited to serve on that committee, or sit at the head table, or buy that bigger house, or have that mother killed, we will be satisfied. But we will not. That's the deceitfulness of sin. The late Welch preacher, Martyn Lloyd-Jones, described it like this:

> Sin never satisfies; it never has done, it never will do; it cannot because it is wrong, it is foul. It never satisfies, although it is always offering satisfaction. Indeed, sin working through lusts never really gives anything at all, but simply takes away. . . .
> Think of the Prodigal Son who is the classical proof to me of all this. There he is, poor fellow, in the field with the husks and the swine. And this is the pregnant phrase of Scripture: "No man gave unto him." But, they had taken a great deal from him, those very people who had emptied his pockets. He had left home with his bit of fortune, and those who became his boon companions. Oh how affable and kind and pleasant they were! How they praised him and toasted his health! He was the finest man in the whole world! Yet they were robbing him the whole time, they took everything he got, and in his penury and his need no man gave to him.

Sin robs us, takes from us, exhausts us mentally, physically, morally, in every respect, and at the end leaves us on the scrap heap, unwanted. It is entirely destructive. It takes away and robs us of character, chastity, purity, honesty, morality, uprightness, delicacy, balance, sensitivity, and everything that is noble in man.[21]

That is not simply a great observation about sin. It is a great observation about affluenza.

In recent days I have learned something about myself. I have learned not only that I have high cholesterol, but that I have affluenza. High affluenza. I can be just as worldly as the next guy. Maybe more so. Sin wants to deceive me into thinking I don't have a problem with affluenza—just as I deceived myself into thinking I didn't have a problem with cholesterol.

In the opening pages of this chapter, I said that children are being sacrificed every day in the civilized jungles of America. They are being sacrificed in my neighborhood and yours. The tendency is to think that someone else down the street has a bad case of affluenza and is sacrificing their kids. That's the deceit of sin. The fact is that Christians can get affluenza so badly that they are not even aware that they are sacrificing their own children in their own Christian homes. Yet it happens every day. That's the deceitfulness of sin: It makes me think that child sacrifice can't happen in my house . . . but it can.

I have come to realize that I have two heart problems. Cholesterol and affluenza. One is a threat to my physical heart, the other a threat to my spiritual heart. Through God's help, I'm working on both of them.

Two hundred years ago Jonathan Edwards faithfully proclaimed the truth of God's Word to his American culture. This is how he stated his objective: "I go to preach with two propositions in mind. First, every person ought to give his life to Christ. Second, whether or not anyone else gives him his life, I will give him mine."

That's the secret to Better Homes and Jungles. And there's one other thing. It's also the antidote to child sacrifice, American style.

Notes

1. Will Durant, *Our Oriental Heritage* (New York: Simon and Schuster, 1954), 50.

2. Francis A. Schaeffer, *The Complete Works of Francis A. Schaeffer: A Christian Worldview, Volume Four, A Christian View of the Church* (Westchester, Ill.: Crossway Books, 1982), 145.

3. Charles Van Doren, *A History of Knowledge: Past, Present, and Future* (New York: Birch Lane Press, 1991), 12-13.

4. Philip Schaff, *History of the Christian Church, Volume V, The Middle Ages* (Grand Rapids: Eerdmans, 1907), 267.

5. Van Doren, *History of Knowledge*, 110.

6. Ibid., 268.

7. *Encyclopedia Britannica*, "Influenza," 12 (Chicago: Encyclopedia Britannica, Inc., 1964), 347.

8. Bruce Shelley, *The Gospel and the American Dream* (Portland, Ore.: Multnomah Press, 1989), 133.

9. Ralph E. Minnear, *Kids Who Have Too Much* (Nashville: Thomas Nelson, 1989), 35.

10. Robert Sure, "Love, Ambition and the Price for a Child's Success," *New York Times*, 17 March 1991, 16Y.

11. Bruce Nichols, "Fierce Competition," *Dallas Morning News*, 10 February 1991, 23A.

12. Robert Sure, "Love, Ambition," 16Y.

13. Ibid.

14. Ibid.

15. *Dallas Morning News*, 23A.

16. Fritz Rienecker and Cleon Rogers, *A Linguistic Key to the Greek New Testament* (Grand Rapids: Zondervan, 1976), 788.

17. David Roper, *The Strength of a Man* (Grand Rapids: Discovery House, 1989), 95.

18. J. Vernon McGee, *Through The Bible, Volume 11, Joshua-Psalm* (Nashville: Thomas Nelson, 1982), 16.

19. Ibid., 17.

20. J. C. Ryle, *Holiness* (Old Tappan, N.J.: Fleming Revell), 5.

21. D. M. Lloyd-Jones, *Darkness and Light* (Grand Rapids: Baker, 1982), 139.

Chapter 4

THE GROSS TRUTH ABOUT NET WORTH

There are two ways to get enough:
One is to accumulate more and more.
The other is to desire less.

G. K. Chesterton

J. Edgar Hoover ran the FBI, no question about it. As a result, almost all of his subordinates were on the lookout for ways to impress their powerful boss.

A young FBI man was put in charge of the FBI's supply department. In an effort to cut some costs and impress his boss, he reduced the size of the office memo paper. One of the new memo sheets soon ended up on Hoover's desk. Hoover took one look at it, determined he didn't like the size of the margins on the paper, and quickly scribbled on the memo, "Watch the borders!"

The memo was passed on through the office. For the next six weeks, it was extremely difficult to enter the United States by road from either Mexico or Canada. The FBI was watching the borders.

Why was the FBI watching the borders? They thought they had received a warning from their chief. But they hadn't. They had transformed an innocuous comment into a solemn warning.

We have a commander-in-chief who is very careful and deliberate in His communication to us. That's why there can be no mistake about the following passages. Each of them has something in common. They each carry a warning—a warning about money.

Do not weary yourself to gain wealth (Proverbs 23:4, NASB).

He who loves money will not be satisfied with money (Ecclesiastes 5:10).

Those who want to get rich fall into temptation and a snare and many foolish and harmful desires which plunge men into ruin and destruction (1 Timothy 6:9, NASB).

Keep your lives free from the love of money and be content with what you have, because God has said, "Never will I leave you; never will I forsake you." So we say with confidence, "The Lord is my helper; I will not be afraid. What can man do to me?" (Hebrews 13:5-6).

The inspired Scriptures give us clear warning from our Lord. And the message is this: when it comes to money, watch the borders. Because He loves us, He lets us know that handling money is risky. If we do not listen to His wisdom and respect the borders He has set up, we can easily come to ruin.

Americans are used to warnings. In recent days I have read warning labels or articles that have alerted me to the following: defective car seats, inhaling fumes at the gas station, opening hot radiators, drinking diet soft drinks, smoking cigarettes, wearing seat belts, and letting small children play with the plastic bags that cover clothes from the dry cleaner. These warnings are all designed to make us aware of potential dangers.

But when was the last time you saw a warning label on a ten dollar bill, a stock certificate, a bank deposit slip or imprinted on a credit card? You certainly will not find these warnings posted in *Money* magazine. Yet that's exactly where they belong. In the February 1991 issue of *Money*, publisher William S. Meyers addressed his subscribers:

If you subscribe to *Money*, you belong to a most exceptional group. Exceptionally ambitious, exceptionally successful and exceptionally affluent.

He then refers to a recent subscriber survey and paints the picture of a typical reader.

You got married sometime after college, and things have gone quite well on the job. You earn a very good living, and you are in a position to make important decisions. You enjoy travel, reading, cooking, music and the theater.

You own two cars, a bicycle, jogging shoes and a whole lot more.

You are active in civic affairs. And oh, yes, there are exactly 2.6 people in your household. Well, not exactly. But you're getting the picture.

Overall, the survey reveals a most accomplished and interesting individual.

Naturally, since *Money* offers solid investment advice, you have a significant portfolio. In order of preference, subscribers hold IRAs, money-market accounts, stocks, mutual funds, CDs and investment real estate.

These assets rest on a firm foundation: a successful career. The great majority of *Money* subscribers have professional or managerial positions. One in six sits on a board of directors, while 22% are in top management.

That kind of earning power means buying power. And here's another area where *Money's* subscribers shine. For example:

• Seven in ten are interested in purchasing ever-higher-tech electronics products;

• Nearly two-thirds own a personal computer;

• Most have traveled abroad recently, averaging three such trips in the past three years.

All in all, an impressive profile. We are pleased that you choose *Money* magazine to play a key role in your continuing success story.[1]

I am reminded of a statement by George Bernard Shaw: "Tell me all my faults as a man. I can stand anything but flattery."

People who have been blessed to this degree don't need flattery. They need a warning. I need a warning and you need a warning. I am an American citizen and I am assuming the same of you. That makes us rich. Perhaps not rich by our standards, but without question we are rich compared to the rest of the world.

I agree with Mr. Meyers. This is quite an impressive profile. I think it was this type of demographic cluster that the Apostle Paul had in mind when he wrote:

> Instruct those who are rich in this present world not to be conceited or to fix their hope on the uncertainty of riches, but on God, who richly supplies us with all things to enjoy.

> Instruct them to do good, to be rich in good works, to be generous and ready to share, storing up for themselves the treasure of a good foundation for the future, so that they may take hold of that which is life indeed (1 Timothy 6:17-19, NASB).

We should make several observations about this letter to the subscribers of *Money*. First, we should observe that they are not just ambitious, successful, and affluent, but that they are *exceptionally* ambitious, *exceptionally* successful, and *exceptionally* affluent. In a group like that, I would think it would be easy to become *exceptionally* proud.

Second, their households consist of exactly 2.6 people. As Mr. Meyers says, "Well, not exactly. But you're getting the picture." Yes, I think we are. Assuming that 2.6 people includes a husband and wife (and in this day and age, that is no longer a safe assumption) that leaves room in the children category for .6. Well, not exactly, but I think you're getting the picture. The picture I'm getting is that children are not a high priority for the "typical" reader of *Money*.

Third, note that after mentioning personal investment preferences, the brochure states, "These assets rest on a firm foundation: a successful career." As I read those words I thought of a man in his early thirties, married, with three children and a high level position with a nationally known company. His base salary is just slightly over $100,000. Or at least it was. He was laid off just days before this past Christmas. So much for a firm foundation.

Fourth, in closing the article Mr. Meyers hopes that the magazine will be playing "a key role in your continuing financial success story." That is a large assumption. A very large assumption. This morning I read in the "What's News" column of the *Wall Street Journal*:

- Hemorrhaging Money, Ford Cuts Spending And May Sell Assets;
- Delta posted a $207.8 million quarterly loss;
- Southwestern Bell reported a 10 percent drop in fourth-quarter profit;
- Shawmut National recorded a $215.7 million fourth-period loss and plans to cut its work force 10 percent;
- Staff reductions are a major part of Citicorp's plan to reduce annual operating costs by 1.5 billion.[2]

It doesn't take a genius to figure out that this kind of economic news is going to be a major obstacle in the "continuing financial success stories" of a number of people.

That's why there needs to be a warning. A timely warning can enable a person to make a wise decision and avoid impending disaster. I think Dennis Levine wishes he had been warned.

By his own admission, Levine was exceptionally ambitious, exceptionally successful, and exceptionally affluent. And it ruined his life.

> Dennis Levine made history. The disclosure of his misdeeds exposed those of Ivan Boesky, his illicit partner, and Boesky in turn led the government to Michael Milken and Drexel Burnham Lambert. The stocks Levine bought and sold through off-shore bank accounts were mainly of target companies in soon-to-be-announced mergers . . . he made his largest single insider-trading profit on securities of Nabisco brands. The SEC alleges that he bought 150,000 Nabisco shares some three weeks before the company announced merger talks with R. J. Reynolds in 1985. When the stock's price rose, Levine sold for a $2.7 million profit.[3]

Levine came from a good home, had a loving wife with one child and one more on the way. He came from a middle-class background and made his own way without any help. He worked hard, took classes in the evening, and eventually earned an MBA.

So what was a guy like this doing in Lewisburg Federal Prison in Pennsylvania?

Levine tells it in his own words with the hope that his experience will warn someone else. That's why he now lectures in colleges and universities. He is trying to warn students of the dangers inherent in a bad case of mushrooms. Success, ambition, and money nearly destroyed his life. Levine writes:

> Why would somebody who's making over $1 million a year start trading on inside information? That's the wrong question. . . . When I started trading on nonpublic information in 1978, I wasn't making a million. I was a twenty-five-year-old trainee at Citibank with a $19,000 annual salary. I was wet behind the ears, impatient, burning with ambition. . . . Eventually insider trading became an addiction for me. It was just so easy. In seven years, I built $39,750 (gathered from family loans and credit card cash advances) into $11.5 million, and all it took was a 20 second phone call to my offshore bank a couple of times a month . . . my account was growing at 125 percent a year compounded.
>
> And Wall Street was crazy in those days. These were the 1980s, remember, the decade of excess, greed, and materialism. I became

a go-go guy, consumed by the high-pressure, ultracompetitive world of investment banking. I was helping my clients make tens and even hundreds of millions of dollars. . . . The daily exposure to such deals, the pursuit of larger and larger transactions, and the numbing effect of 60-to 100-hour work weeks helped erode my values and distort my judgment.

At the root of my compulsive trading was an inability to set limits. Perhaps it's worth noting that my legitimate success stemmed from the same root. My ambition was so strong it went beyond rationality, and I gradually lost sight of what constitutes ethical behavior. At each new level of success I set higher goals, imprisoning myself in a cycle from which I saw no escape. When I became a senior vice president, I wanted to be a managing director, and when I became a managing director, I wanted to be a client. If I was making $100,000 a year, I thought, I can make $200,000. And if I made $1 million, I can make $3 million. And so it went.

Competitive jealousy is normal in business. Everybody wants to make more than the guy down the hall. It is the same in investment banking, but the numbers have more zeroes. Only a small percentage of the people these firms hire at the entry level of associate go on to make partner, and as the pyramid narrows, the competition grows ever more intense. By the time I made partner at Drexel, I was out of control. . . . We all regularly put in time on weekends and after 7 or 8 P.M., when the partners usually knocked off for the evening. The hours were so obscene that my family ribbed me about being a wage slave. But I loved my work. I realized, hey, I'm doing this, and I'm doing it well.[4]

In light of Mr. Levine's candid account, let's go over those warnings one more time.

Do not weary yourself to gain wealth (Proverbs 23:4).

There is nothing wrong with having riches if God allows them to come your way. It is wrong, however, to expend all of your energy in the quest for more and more. Some economic systems prohibit a person from improving their lot in life. That is wrong as well. Different economic systems operate on diverse principles.

As a public service, please note the following pocketbook guide to economic systems:

- Socialism: If you have two cows, you give one to your neighbor.
- Communism: If you have two cows, you give them to the government, then the government gives you some milk.
- Fascism: If you have two cows, you keep the cows and give the

milk to the government; then the government sells you some milk.
- Nazism: If you have two cows, the government shoots you and keeps the cows.
- New Dealism: If you have two cows, you shoot one and milk the other, then you pour the milk down the drain.
- Capitalism: If you have two cows, sell one and buy a bull.[5]

Capitalism is not a perfect system by any means. But it does give you the opportunity to improve your lot in life and the lot of others. But it can be wearying if one does not build limits into his life. John Piper comments:

> We live in a society in which many legitimate businesses depend on large concentrations of capital. You can't build a new manufacturing plant without millions of dollars in equity. Therefore, financial officers in big businesses often have the responsibility to build reserves, for example, by selling shares to the community. When the Bible condemns the desire to get rich, it is not necessarily condemning a business which aims to expand and therefore seeks larger capital reserves. The officers of the business may be greedy for more personal wealth, or they may have larger, nobler motives of how their expanded productivity will benefit people.[6]

Levine admits that his motives were not noble. Pure and simple, he wanted to get rich. So he wearied himself to gain riches. He had to work unbelievable hours during the week, and then go back on weekends. He himself called these hours "numbing" and blamed those numbing hours for helping to erode his values and distort his judgment. To his credit, he now tells other businessmen about the importance of spending time with their families. He wearied himself to gain riches, and found that it was not worth the effort. By the way, how is your schedule these days?

> He who loves money will not be satisfied with money (Ecclesiastes 5:10, NASB).

Levine found out that making $100,000 a year wasn't enough. Neither was $300,000 or $1 million or $3 million. How much are you currently making? How much do you think it would take to give you a sense of satisfaction? Levine discovered that no matter how much more he made, it did not bring satisfaction. He found out firsthand what Solomon had discovered thousands of years ago. Money cannot bring satisfaction. But there is another warning:

Those who want to get rich fall into temptation and a snare and many foolish and harmful desires which plunge men into ruin and destruction (1 Timothy 6:9, NASB).

Do you want to *Think and Grow Rich* as the popular book title promises? Then be very careful. C. H. Spurgeon put it this way: "It is a very serious thing to grow rich. Of all the temptations to which God's children are exposed, it is the worst, because it is the one they do not dread. Therefore, it is the more subtle temptation."

Wanting to get rich is a very subtle temptation. And the reason it is subtle is that we think it can't hurt us. The fact is that it can destroy us.

Levine's transparent account tells us that the pursuit of more and more money was a snare. His desires became foolish and harmful. And he was plunged into ruin and destruction. According to Levine, "Saying goodbye to your family is painful enough, but try explaining to a five-year-old why Daddy is going to prison."

Dennis Levine is not the first man to discover that the desire to be rich can plunge men into ruin and destruction:

In 1923, seven men who had made it to the top of the pyramid met together at the Edgewater Hotel in Chicago. Collectively, they controlled more wealth than the entire United States Treasury, and for years the media had held them up as examples of success.

Who were they? Charles Schwab, president of the world's largest independent steel company; Arthur Cutten, the greatest wheat speculator of his day; Richard Whitney, president of the New York Stock Exchange; Albert Fall, a member of the President's Cabinet; Jesse Livermore, the greatest bear on Wall Street; Leon Fraser, president of the International Bank of Settlement; and Ivar Kruegger, head of the world's largest monopoly. What happened to them? Schwab and Cutten both died broke; Whitney spent years of his life in Sing Sing penitentiary; Fall also spent years in prison but was released so he could die at home; and the others, Livermore, Fraser, and Kruegger, committed suicide.[7]

Paul was right. Those who want to get rich don't realize they are flirting with ruin and destruction. And there is one other thing they usually don't think about. The scriptures speak clearly about the uncertainty of riches. We hear so much today about "financial security." There is nothing wrong with financial planning. But there is everything wrong with thinking that your financial planning will bring you security for your future. Your security for your future rests in Jesus Christ—*exclusively*.

What are the chances that you or I will ever amass the financial portfolio of Schwab or Cutten? The chances are slim and none, and as they say in Texas, Slim just left town. Do you think those two men had any idea in 1923 when they walked into the Edgewater Hotel that they would die broke? I seriously doubt it.

From what I can gather from Dennis Levine's testimony, I don't believe he would claim to have a personal relationship with Jesus Christ. But I do believe he would agree with the wisdom of these warnings. He discovered the truth about them firsthand.

> Keep your lives free from the love of money and be content with what you have, because God has said, "Never will I leave you; never will I forsake you." So we say with confidence, "The Lord is my helper; I will not be afraid; What can man do to me?" (Hebrews 13:5-6).

Stacey Woods knew all about financial security, but he didn't learn it on Wall Street. He learned it from his parents. His parents established churches in the outback of Australia. In his biography, this founder of the InterVarsity Christian Fellowship in America tells of the faith of his father, who taught him much about the security of trusting in God:

> Father had a profound trust in God and his promises. He took Matthew 6:33 literally ["But seek first His kingdom and His righteousness; and all these things shall be added to you"]: God had promised to meet his need. He never had a salary, never took up an offering for his ministry nor authorized anyone else to do so, never asked anyone for personal support.
>
> This quiet confidence on the part of both my parents, for Mother stood one hundred percent with Father, made a deep impression on me. Trusting God for everything was part of our life. . . .
>
> Once in his caravan days Father and his fellow worker had finished up every crumb of food for breakfast. And neither of them had a cent to buy more. It came time for the midday meal. To the astonishment of the younger man, Father said, "Let us lay the table for dinner."

"But we have no food," exclaimed his companion.

"God has promised that we shall not go hungry. We must honor him by our faith in his promise."

The table was set, glasses filled with water.

"Let us sit down and give thanks for our meal," said my father. Heads were bowed and thanks returned.

As the prayer ended, a knock sounded on the caravan door. There stood a woman they had never seen before. "Me and my man are having a chicken dinner and thought you fellers might like some." She had walked more than a quarter of a mile across the fields bringing that chicken dinner with all the "fixins."[8]

Woods then makes this comment to all of us:

The trend of government is to undergird us with material securities from the cradle to the grave, providing all kinds of insurances: health, old-age, education, unemployment, and so on. In addition, we insure ourselves against fire, earthquake, hurricane, accident and old-age. These safeguards are not wrong, but they can very easily become a serious hindrance to our complete trust in God. Undoubtedly, if our debts are paid and our refrigerator full, if we have money in the bank, we have the tendency to feel secure in ourselves and our need of God is less. Herein lies the danger. My greatest need is to feel and know my need of God every hour.[9]

I am writing these words in January 1991. There is a genuine concern in this country about the state of the economy. We have been at war with Iraq for one week, and everyone is hoping that it will be a short operation. But no one knows for sure.

It was clear before we got into this war that we were in a recession. Some economists say it will be short, but no one really knows. People are worried about their jobs. Having a job today is no guarantee that you will have one next week, no matter how high up the ladder you are.

Many people can identify with a recent *Peanuts* cartoon strip. Violet comes upon Charlie Brown and Linus one day, both of whom look frightened. She asks them, "What are you two so worried about?" Charlie Brown answers, "We're afraid of the future." Violet thinks for a moment, then asks, "Well, what are you afraid of? Tomorrow? Friday? Next week? Anything in particular?" "No," replies Linus, taking his thumb out of his mouth, "We're worried about everything. Yes, our worrying is very broad-minded."[10]

No matter how broad minded you are in your worrying, the truth is still sufficient. "God has said, 'Never will I leave you; never will I forsake you.' So we say with confidence, 'The Lord is my helper; I will not be afraid. What can man do to me?' " (Hebrews 13:5b-6). That's a relatively easy verse to memorize. It's a little more difficult to believe it and act upon it.

Let me ask you a question. Do you really believe that the Lord will never fail you or forsake you? Then why don't you relax a bit as you ponder your future? He knows what you are up against and how fragile your situation may be. And He has a solution that is already signed and sealed. It will be delivered at the right time.

We all enjoy hearing stories like the one about Stacy Woods's father, but most of us would never choose to put ourselves in such a dependent situation. Perhaps I am writing to someone recently unemployed. Your benefits are about to run out and you see no prospect of things changing. May I encourage you with the thought that you are in an enviable position? You are about to be in a situation that requires complete dependence on the Lord. He will come through for you! If we are never in a state of need, we will miss the tremendous experience of seeing God provide a way and an answer that will astonish us.

YOU GOTTA SERVE SOMEBODY

A number of years ago, Bob Dylan wrote a song you may remember:

> You may be an ambassador to England or France,
> You may like to gamble, you might like to dance,
> You may be the heavyweight champion of the world,
> You might be a socialite with a long string of pearls
> But you're gonna have to serve somebody . . .
> May be a construction worker, working on a home,
> Might be living in a mansion, you might live in a dome,
> You may own guns and you may even own tanks,
> You may be somebody's landlord, you may even own banks,
> But you're gonna have to serve somebody . . .[11]

That's the root idea of Luke 16:13 where Jesus said;

No servant can serve two masters. Either he will hate the one and love the other, or he will be devoted to the one and despise the other. You cannot serve both God and Money. *The Pharisees, who loved money, heard all this and were sneering at Jesus* (italics mine).

The Pharisees chose whom they would serve. They would serve money, because they loved money. On another occasion, a group of Pharisees were trying to trap Jesus.

Hearing that Jesus had silenced the Sadducees, the Pharisees got together. One of them, an expert in the law, tested him with this question: "Teacher, which is the greatest commandment in the Law?" Jesus replied: " 'Love the Lord your God with all your heart and with all your soul and with all your mind.' This is the first and greatest commandment. And the second is like it: 'Love your neighbor as yourself.' All the Law and the Prophets hang on these two commandments" (Matthew 22:34-40).

You can either love God with all your heart and with all your soul and with all your mind, or you can love something else with all of your heart, soul, and mind. The Pharisees wanted to give the impression that they were lovers of God. Yet, they were not. They were lovers of money. They had made the decision.

We are free to choose whom or what we will serve. In the final analysis, we choose to serve that which we love.

BRINGING HOME THE BACON

In 1893, Richard D. Armour was worth fifty million dollars. That's a lot of money today; it was much more back then. He had built his meat packing business from the ground up until he had fifteen thousand employees. Despite his enormous wealth, Armour arose at 5:00 each morning and drove to the plant. There he stayed, this mighty transformer of meat into money, until 6:00 in the evening, at which time he went home for dinner, followed by a 9:00 bedtime. "I have no other interest in my life but my business," he told an interviewer. "I do not love the money. What I do love is the getting of it."[12]

We serve what we love. Armour loved making money more than money itself. But he still had to serve somebody. In his case, he served the love of acquiring money. Now the question is this: what are you serving? We serve what we love. So perhaps the better question is this: what do you love? What is the primary attachment in your life? There is only one sane answer to that question in light of eternity.

> . . . Picture 269 people entering eternity in a plane crash in the Sea of Japan. Before the crash there is a noted politician, a millionaire corporate executive, a playboy and his playmate, a missionary kid on the way back from visiting grandparents.
>
> After the crash they stand before God utterly stripped of Mastercards, checkbooks, credit lines, image clothes, how-to-succeed books, and Hilton reservations. Here are the politician, the executive, the playboy, and the missionary kid, all on level ground with nothing, absolutely nothing in their hands, possessing only what they brought in their hearts. How absurd and tragic the lovers of money will seem on that day. . . . [13]

A profound phrase has stuck with me over the years. "It is better to fail in a cause that will ultimately succeed than to succeed in a cause that will ultimately fail." There are many in our culture who have chosen to serve that which will ultimately fail. If money is temporary, if money is uncertain, then why devote your life to pursuing it as Malcolm Forbes did? It is no wonder that Forbes once said, "If there is a next life, people like me had better hope the devil is not as bad off as he's painted." What a tragic commentary on one's own life. A life spent serving money.

The movie *Wall Street* contained an insightful comment: "The problem with money is that it makes you do things you don't want to do." That's what bad masters do. They enslave their followers. That's the pity of choosing to serve money.

AN UNUSUAL REQUEST

Are you familiar with a man in the Bible named Agur? He prayed one of the most unusual prayers in all of the Bible. It concerned money. The prayer to which I refer is recorded in Proverbs 30:7-8:

> Two things I asked of Thee,
> Do not refuse me before I die:
> Keep deception and lies far from me,
> Give me neither poverty nor riches . . . (NASB)

Agur asked God to bless him by granting him two requests.

The first request was that God might enable him to be a man of truth. He asked God to keep deception and lies far from him. That was a wise prayer.

The next request is the unusual one. What is unusual is that Agur asks God *not* to give him two things. First, he asks that God not give him poverty. We would all say amen to that. But in the same breath, he asks God *not* to give him riches. You won't hear too many amens on that one.

Why would Agur ask God to not give him riches? Why didn't he just practice "positive confession" as some television evangelists encourage us to do? One of these religious media figures recently saw a beautiful home and wanted to buy it. "I began to see that I already had authority over that house and authority over the money I needed to purchase it. I said, 'In the name of Jesus, I take authority over the money I need. (I called out the specific amount.) I command you to come to me . . . in Jesus' name. Ministering spirits, you go and cause it to come.' "[14]

That would be funny if it weren't so pathetic. Nowhere in Scripture are Christians told that they have authority over money. Nowhere in Scripture are Christians told that they have authority over angels like we have authority over a basset hound. We don't command the angels to go and fetch anything. And what if two different people are commanding the angels to go and fetch the same house? Then what happens? Maybe you could command an angel to fetch Monty Hall and he would let you trade for what's behind door number 2.

This sort of teaching about money and wealth is unbiblical, it is out of balance, and it appeals to the greed that lies deep within all of us. It is simply wrong. I can tell you this: if Agur were around today, he sure wouldn't buy it.

I appreciate David Roper's perspective:

Early Christians would have abhorred our pursuit of ease and affluence. Back then no one would have believed that becoming a Christian could place a man among the rich and famous. Today for some it's considered a divine right. Some say that sickness, poverty, and infamy are signs of unbelief and that God wants us all to be healthy, wealthy, and wise. Apparently then, the only victory that demonstrates closeness to God is full healing and circumstantial happiness. If only it were so.

Such a theology of success simply isn't so; God saves greater things for us than mere earthly happiness. Unscriptural and unrealistic expectations can plunge us into despair and unbelief and cause us to ignore what's really taking place."[15]

What was Agur's problem? Why does he ask God not to give him riches? Why doesn't he wise up and take authority over the money he wants and command the angels to go and get it for him? May I remind you that Agur writes under the inspiration of the Holy Spirit. Yet the message that constantly bombards us from so many superficial thinkers is that we should ask—no, that's not right, we should virtually *command*—the riches to come to us.

Agur in essence is saying, "Dear God, please, I ask of you, whatever you do, don't give me riches." Again, why would Agur make such a request? The answer is simple. Agur is watching his borders. On the one hand, he asks that God not give him poverty. That's one border. On the other, he asks God not to give him riches. That's another border. Agur wanted to stay within his borders. He didn't want poverty, he didn't want riches, he just wanted enough to make his mortgage and car payment, put some away for retirement, and get the kids through college.

As I read it, Agur was asking God to keep him in the middle. Agur was the original cheerleader for the middle class. When was the last time you heard anyone express a desire to be middle-class? Agur was asking for middle-class because Agur was watching his borders.

But why was he watching his borders? What infiltrator did he fear? What threat did he perceive? He doesn't leave us guessing:

Keep falsehood and lies far from me;
> give me neither poverty nor riches,
> but give me only my daily bread.
Otherwise, I may have too much and disown you
> *and say, "Who is the LORD?"*
Or I may become poor and steal,
> *and so dishonor the name of my God*
> (Proverbs 30:8-9).

At the heart of Agur's odd request is an overpowering desire to stay close to God. Agur was a wise man. He knew that "stuff" can turn a man's heart away from God. Having too much of it can make a man proud and deceive him into thinking he doesn't need God (remember Malcolm Forbes?); having too little of it can make a man desperate and deceive him into thinking God doesn't care about him. But notice this: the worst thing, *either way*, is that God loses the central place in life which He must occupy.

We don't know much about the identity of Agur, but it is safe to surmise that he either was a contemporary of Solomon or one who lived not too long after Solomon. Is it not possible that one of the reasons he asks God not to give him riches is that he knew firsthand what riches had done to Solomon? Riches, among other things, destroyed Solomon. And the ruin of Solomon was an enormous lesson to Agur. Perhaps as he pondered the end of Solomon, he thought, "Dear God, please don't give me riches." Despite his God-given wisdom, Solomon couldn't handle riches. He couldn't stay within the borders.

So if riches got a hold of Solomon's heart and caused him to fall, what makes us think we are not susceptible? What makes us think we will do any better? Ralph Waldo Emerson was correct when he said sometimes "money costs too much."

> For the love of money is a root of all sorts of evil, and some by longing for it have wandered away from the faith, and pierced themselves with many a pang. But *flee* from these things . . .

Are you staying within your spiritual borders when it comes to money, or have you been slipping over the border without a passport? What are you pursuing? Are you pursuing Christ or are you pursuing riches? Are you fleeing from riches or are you flying toward riches?

If you are interested in the ultimate financial portfolio, here is the prospectus for genuine financial security: Seek ye *first* the kingdom of God, and all of these things shall be added unto you.

In your heart of hearts, what are you seeking?

Notes

1. William S. Meyers, "Publisher's Letter," *Money*, February 1991, 4.

2. "What's News," *Wall Street Journal*, Vol. LXXVII, No. 17, 24 January 1991, 1.

3. "The Inside Story of an Inside Trader," *Fortune*, 21 May 1990, 80.

4. Ibid.

5. *Disciplemaker Newsletter*, author and date unknown, ed. Monte Unger.

6. John Piper, *Desiring God* (Portland, Ore.: Multnomah Press, 1986), 155.

7. Donald McCullough, *Waking From The American Dream* (Downer's Grove: InterVarsity Press, 1988), 77.

8. Stacy Woods, *Some Ways of God* (Downer's Grove: InterVarsity Press, 1975), 15.

9. Ibid.

10. Archibald Hart, *The Success Factor* (Old Tappan, NJ: Revell, 1984), 96.

11. Bob Dylan, *Gotta Serve Somebody* (New York: Special Rider Music). Used by permission.

12. "The Forgotten Four Hundred: Chicago's First Millionaires," *American Heritage*, November 1987, 37.

13. Piper, *Desiring God*, 156.

14. Dave Hunt, *The Seduction of Christianity* (Eugene, Ore.: Harvest House, 1985), 101.

15. David H. Roper, *The Strength of a Man* (Grand Rapids: Discovery House, 1989), 65.

Chapter 5

*T*he Continental Provide

*No woman should be authorized to stay at home
and raise her children. . . . Women should not have that choice,
precisely because if there is such a choice,
too many women will make that one.*

Feminist leader Simone de Beauvoir

A lot of rich Texans went broke in the 1980s. But there are still a few rich Texans left. One of them was recently talking to a banker in New York. After several minutes of conversation, the Texan took a liking to the New Yorker. "I've got a great idea," he said. "Why don't I send my jet up to New York this weekend to pick up you and your wife? We'd like to have you join us at our son's ranch outside of Austin. He's got 100,000 acres of land stocked with quarter horses, purebred cattle, and exotic game. Yep, I'm real proud of the boy. He earned it all by himself."

"It sounds like your son has been very successful for a young man," replied the banker. "Just out of curiosity, how old is your son?"

"He's eight," replied the Texan.

"Eight!" said the shocked banker. "How on earth did an eight-year-old boy earn enough money to buy a ranch like that?"

"He got four A's and one B," replied the Texan.

*T*HE CONTINENTAL PROVIDE

We have just finished a chapter filled with warnings about money. Someone out there may be thinking, *Wait a minute! All of these warnings on money are well and good, but don't I have to provide for my family?* Of course you do. I have met men all over this continent who are working hard to provide for their families. It's a phenomenon I call the Continental Provide. But there is more to the Continental Provide than most men realize.

Most men think that providing for their families means they provide financially, and that is true. But that's not all it means. Too many men think that if they bring home the bacon they have completely fulfilled their responsibilities. Nothing could be further from the truth, as we will see in just a few minutes. A man is to provide for his home. And he is to provide in at least four ways. In my estimation, a man who only provides financially for his family is not a success, no matter how much money he makes. The truly successful man provides well for his family in each of the following four areas.

1. The man is out in the jungle to provide financially.

Let's get back to the fundamentals. If you have a family, you work in order to provide for that family. You are not out there to get promoted, or to find significance, or to climb the corporate ladder. You are out there to feed, clothe, and shelter your family.

> Once upon a time, one's career clock wasn't as complex as it is today. A person started at a job and tried to run as fast and as far as he could. He galloped uphill and ran straight ahead. Then he got a gold watch and disappeared into his hothouse. That was back when America was ruled by the work ethic . . . the work ethic was eventually supplanted by the career ethic, which in turn gave way to the fulfillment ethic. Says the fulfillment ethic: Jobs are no longer just to put food on the table; they exist to serve our emotional needs and to further our spiritual goals. Once it was hard work that built character; now it's the right work.[1]

Gentlemen, if you are out in the jungle, it is for one basic reason: you are there to provide for your family. Paul emphasized this in 1 Timothy 5:8: "But if any one does not provide for his own, and especially for those of his household, he has denied the faith, and is worse than an unbeliever."

The context of that passage concerns the needs of widows in the church. I conclude from this that not only am I responsible for my immediate family, but for my parents and my wife's parents as they get on in years. God intends that I meet the needs of those who raised me, while at the same time caring for the little ones I am raising.

That's why you are out in the jungle. You are providing and planning not only for today, but for the day when you may have to provide for your parents. In other words, you are out in the jungle to provide financially for the needs of your family.

Financial planning of that caliber requires good biblical advice. I highly recommend Ron Blue's excellent book, *Mastering Your Money*. It provides a sane and biblical approach to financial planning that is the best I have seen.

2. When you come home from the jungle, you are to provide emotionally.

I don't remember where I got this, but I have never forgotten it. It came from a guy who played basketball for John Wooden at UCLA. UCLA had a lock on college basketball from 1964 through 1975. During that eleven-year span, UCLA won the national title nine times.

This ballplayer was recounting his first day of practice under Wooden. Everyone was awed by the presence of this living legend. But they were completely shocked when he came into the locker room and spent several minutes showing these high school all-Americans the proper way to put on their socks and lace up their shoes.

They thought Wooden was nuts. They knew how to put on their socks and tie their shoes! They weren't a group of kindergartners; they were a group of talented college freshman. Why would a legend like Wooden be concerned about socks?

The answer is simple. If a player gets blisters from socks that are not smooth or shoes that are not correctly fitted, then that player cannot play up to his ability. Wooden didn't overlook anything. Not even blisters.

Men are to provide for their families not just financially, but emotionally. That means that they look to prevent the emotional blisters that can develop as we chafe against other people. A successful man makes sure that there are no emotional blisters developing in the lives of his wife or children. He is there to smooth things out and to offer strong support. He is quick to let each member of his family know that they are important and valuable.

But if a man spends the vast majority of his waking hours during the week and on the weekend providing financially, how will he ever hope to provide emotionally? The answer is, he can't. But he should have enough money to send his family to a counselor for family therapy.

3. When you come home from the jungle, you are to provide morally.

By the way, what time do you have? I have 12:23 P.M. When you set your watch, by what do you set it? I usually set my watch by the local news radio station. But let me ask you a question. What if the radio station has the wrong time? Who sets the clock at the radio station? It is important to know how the clocks at the radio station are calibrated because everyone else takes their time from the station. If the station is wrong, then all of the listeners are wrong.

In the home, the father is the moral atomic clock. Everyone else sets their moral watch according to him. If he is off morally, then they will be off morally. If he has the correct moral time, then they will have the correct time.

If a man spends all of his time providing financially, he will not have the time to provide morally. And if you are not the one setting your child's moral clock, then who will? Maybe you could get your son a subscription to *Dirt* magazine.

Lang Communications, Inc. is throwing a new magazine named *Dirt* at the market for teenage boys, hoping to duplicate its success with the teen-age girls magazine *Sassy*. . . . Following *Sassy*'s lead could bring some instant controversy. When *Sassy* was launched with a circulation of 250,000 in 1988, Ms. Pratt as editor made it clear that the magazine would speak candidly about issues facing young women, such as contraception and homosexual relationships. . . . With the exception of *Boy's Life*, there are few magazines directed solely at that male age group. Jane Pratt, editor in chief of *Sassy*, said that *Dirt* would contain articles that are both "irreverent and candid," much as *Sassy* has in its three years . . .

Sassy publisher, Bobbie Halfin, said advertising categories for *Dirt* would include footwear, sportswear, electronics, recorded music, and toiletries. *Dirt*, however, will not take ads for cigarettes or liquor, she added.[2]

So they won't take ads for cigarettes or liquor. How moral of them.

You can spend the vast majority of your time providing financially. But who is going to provide morally for your family? Especially in an age when *Boy's Life* is being replaced by literal *Dirt*.

4. When you come home from the jungle, you are to provide spiritually.

The husband is the spiritual leader of the home. He is responsible for the spiritual well-being and nourishment of his family. He must become aggressively involved in his own spiritual development so that he can lead from the maturity of his own life. Deuteronomy 6:1-2,4-7 gives the pattern for spiritual leadership in the home:

> Now this is the commandment, the statutes and the judgments which the LORD your God has commanded me to teach you, that you might do them in the land where you are going over to possess it, so that you and your son and your grandson might fear the LORD your God, to keep all His statutes and His commandments, which I command you, all the days of your life, and that your days may be prolonged.
>
> Hear, O Israel! The LORD is our God, the LORD is one! And you shall love the LORD your God with all your heart and with all your soul and with all your might. And these words, which I am commanding you today, shall be on your heart; and you shall teach them diligently to your sons and shall talk of them when you sit in your house and when you walk by the way and when you lie down and when you rise up (NASB).

Notice that this instruction is given to *fathers.* That is important. Men are to take an active role in teaching their children the things of the Lord. They are to do that in both formal and informal situations. Too many men have left this side of leadership to their wives. But Deuteronomy 6 wasn't addressed primarily to wives. It was written to husbands.

Unfortunately, it's easy to get so caught up with financial accumulation that a man begins to forget the Lord and that he is to provide spiritually in his home. That is such a problem that God warned the men of Israel about it in the same context as the above text:

> Then it shall come about when the LORD your God brings you into the land which He swore to your fathers, Abraham, Isaac and Jacob, to give you, great and splendid cities which you did not

build, and houses full of all good things which you did not fill, and hewn cisterns which you did not dig, vineyards and olive trees which you did not plant, and you shall eat and be satisfied, then watch yourself, lest you forget the LORD who brought you from the land of Egypt, out of the house of slavery (Deuteronomy 6:10-12).

PROVISION AND CARE: THE TWO NON-NEGOTIABLES

So far I have directed my comments to the men because that's where I believe this discussion must start. But having done that, I'd like to backtrack a bit and speak to both men and women. Everything I have just written depends upon a statement I know is likely to offend a number of people. Before I make it, I would like you to consider this point: this same statement, if made twenty-five years ago, probably would have offended no one. The statement is this: *In the home, the man is to be the primary provider and the wife is to be the primary caregiver.*

Now we need to make some immediate clarifications. First, please note the word *primary*. I want to head off a problem that could quickly get out of hand. When I say that the man is the primary provider, that does not mean that a man is off the hook when it comes to other family responsibilities. I hope I've already made that clear, but let me underscore the point. Although the *primary* responsibility for care in the family falls to the wife, the husband can and must participate. The modern idea of a man leaving his career to stay at home and raise the kids while mom goes off to work is completely antithetical to God's plan for the family.

I also need to clarify that although the woman is to be the primary caregiver, that does not mean she cannot or should not participate in the financial provision of the home. When a couple has small children, it may be necessary for her to work part-time in order to help make ends meet, but that should not be her primary role. It should be his. Please note the word *primary*. I am using the word in the sense of "chiefly," "largely," or "mostly."

According to the scriptural plan, the man is chiefly responsible for a family's physical provision and the woman is chiefly responsible for its caregiving. This has been God's plan from the beginning. Man was designed to be the primary provider and woman was designed to be the primary caregiver. That was the blueprint, and it's still the blueprint.

Why is this true?

It is true because of the basic structure that God built into families. What is a family? What was God's original blueprint? What did God have in mind when he brought Adam and Eve together? James Hurley writes:

> To end the loneliness of the man and to join him in ruling the earth to the glory of God, God shaped a woman from the flesh of Adam. God's calling to the race came to the two of them, "Increase in number, fill the earth and subdue it" (Genesis 1:28). The loving companionship of the two would issue, in due course, in the birth of children and mankind would become a community serving God through their love and service of him and one another.[3]

When you look at the components of a family, you find that a family has two basic needs:

- A family needs provision.
- A family needs care.

Remember how the FBI was watching the borders? Here are two borders that every husband and wife must watch carefully if they have been given the gift of children. I must watch the border of provision and I must watch the border of care.

These two commodities must be provided. They are non-negotiables. God has ordained that the man's primary responsibility is to meet his family's physical needs, while the woman's primary responsibility is to meet her family's need for nurture and care.

If a new business were to be started by two entrepreneurs in the computer field, it might be decided two essential areas must be covered if the business is to succeed: research and development. One is assigned the primary responsibility of doing research, the other is given the area of development. Without research, there is nothing to develop. Without development, all the research in the world will go to waste. Both are necessary and important. The same is true in the family.

In Genesis, God assigned Adam the responsibility of working to meet the physical needs of the family, while Eve was given the primary responsibility to care for the family. This is seen clearly in the curses that each received after both sinned against God. Three curses were given in Genesis: one to the man, one to the woman, and one to the serpent. For our purposes, we will look briefly only at the curses upon the man and woman. To the woman, God said this:

> I will greatly multiply your pain in childbirth,
> In pain you shall bring forth children;
> Yet your desire shall be for your husband
> and he shall rule over you (Genesis 3:16, NASB).

The curse on the woman revolved around her primary function, birthing and nurturing children. To the man, God said:

> Cursed is the ground because of you;
> In toil you shall eat of it,
> All the days of your life.
> Both thorns and thistles it shall grow for you;
> And you shall eat the plants of the field;
> By the sweat of your face you shall eat bread,
> Till you return to the ground,—
> Because from it you were taken;
> For you are dust, and to dust you shall return
> (Genesis 3:17-19, NASB).

Likewise, the curse on the man focused upon his primary function, making physical provision for the family.

It should be noted that the respective responsibilities of provision and care were given to the man and woman *before* the entrance of sin into the world. The significance of the curses is that they would make Adam and Eve's responsibilities more difficult to perform.

The essential point here is that there are two necessary and vital components that go into the making of a family. Neither can be ignored because both are crucial. That's why God ordained that the husband oversee one area and the wife the other.

We see the same teaching in the New Testament. In 1 Timothy 5:8, the apostle Paul gives this instruction about a man's provision:

> But if any one does not provide for his own, and especially for

those of his household, he has denied the faith, and is worse than
an unbeliever (NASB).

In 1 Timothy 5:14, Paul puts the emphasis on caring when he
addresses young widows:

> So I counsel younger widows to marry, to have children, to *man-age* their homes.

The Greek term, *oikodespoteo*, translated as "manage," is a
forceful word.[4] It insists that the home must be a priority. Women
are to manage their careers when they have children at home,
they are to manage their households. Families must be cared for,
and proper care takes a tremendous amount of management.

Dr. George Knight has pointed out that the woman described
in Proverbs 31 is a beautiful example of this principle. This
woman was incredibly competent. She was a genuine
entrepreneur and a gifted manager. But notice that the focal point
of her activity was in the sphere of the home. Her family was not
neglected as she sought to find meaning in a career outside the
home. On the contrary, she is described in verse 27 as a woman
who

> looks well to the ways of her household, and she does not eat the
> bread of idleness. Her children rise up and bless her; her husband
> also. . . .

Why do her children and husband bless her? Because she stays
at home and watches Phil and Oprah to her heart's delight?
Obviously not. She doesn't have time for such frivolity. This
woman has a home to care for.

A close reading of the context of Proverbs 31:10-31 makes it
clear that this woman works hard to care for her family. She has
what it takes to be a modern day corporate executive. But her
children bless her because they are cared for. She has chosen to
use her gifts and abilities, not to bypass the home, but to carefully
attend to it in detail. No wonder her children praise her! They are
not neglected. They have a mother who cares for them with
everything she has. This woman knows how to manage a home.

In Titus 2:3-5, Paul also describes the caring funciton of the
wife. He writes that the older women are to:

. . . encourage the younger women to love their husbands, to love their children, to be sensible, pure, workers at home, kind, being subject to their own husbands, that the word of God may not be dishonored (vs 4-5).

Please note that Paul instructs women to work, but their work is to be in the context of the home. Why? Because their main responsibility is to provide for the family's nurture and care.

Someone may be thinking that this verse is cultural and applied only to Paul's culture. But this verse is not cultural, it is trans-cultural. What is cultural about a wife loving her husband, or loving her children, or being sensible or kind? If those characteristics are not cultural, then neither is "workers at home" cultural. Scripture cannot be sliced up without regard to context, and the context of this verse is clearly not cultural. Paul did not intend for these instructions to be followed only by Christian women in his culture. These instructions are God's will for every married woman with children in every culture. He desires that *every* family in *every* culture in *every* age is well-cared for by a competent and adequate woman whose heart fully belongs to Jesus Christ. *Every* home is in need of sufficient provision and sufficient care. To that end He has given the man the primary responsibility for provision and the woman the primary responsibility for care.

This is why single parenting is so tough. A single parent is trying to pull off both provision and care at the same time. I commend the countless single parents who are working so hard to provide and care for their children. They are literally doing the work of two people. But it is *so* tough!

The beauty of the scriptural instruction is that when a husband and wife are both working in their divinely appointed areas, the essential needs of the family unit are met. What are these essential needs? Provision and care.

THE CARELESS AMERICAN FAMILY

In my first book, *Point Man*, I explained that until the Industrial Revolution, a man's work was done in the context of the home. Most men were farmers, going from the house to the field to make provision for their families. If a man was a merchant, or a coppersmith, or a printer, his shop usually would be attached to his home. Even though he was the primary provider, he was available and on site to his family. After the onset of the Industrial Revolution, men left the home to work in the factories. This brought about tremendous social upheaval.

Although the man's provision now took place outside of the home, he was still providing while the wife was still giving care inside the home. The basic needs of the family were still being met, although in a much more stressful way.

Our culture is now in tremendous upheaval, because for all intents and purposes, a second Industrial Revolution is upon us. In this revolution millions of women are leaving the home to join their husbands in the workplace. Now both husbands and wives are providing. It's happening all over America. The Continental Provide is proving to be the Continental Divide, for it is dividing family peace and unity from Washington to Florida and from Maine to California.

This is the mistake of our Continental Provide. This new revolution has changed the balance that God ordained for the home, for if the husband and wife are both providing outside the home, then who is going to care for the family? Without realizing it, we have developed a care-less family structure in America. And a care-less family structure is a careless family structure. It is contrary to the scriptures. When a husband and wife both feverishly work in the Continental Provide, they cannot see the emotional hurt of the Continental Divide. Families of ample financial provision are often families of abundant emotional division. The reason for the division is this: they are care-less families.

Our careless family structure has spawned an entirely new American industry known as day *care*. Someone has to care for the children. We all know that. But have we forgotten how desperately important it is that a mother care for her own children?

Families in America are stressed out. It is a jungle out there. Recently after speaking at a church, I had a conversation with a young woman, married with one child. She and her husband are committed Christians. In the first three minutes of our conversation she told me how stressful her life was. She had to work full-time and was putting her young son in day care. She told me how hard it was to put him there for eight to ten hours a day. It was hard for her to hold back the tears as she conveyed her concerns for her child. She said she hoped to stop working and return home sometime the following year.

That afternoon, the person taking me back to my hotel stopped at a friend's home to drop off a package. We pulled up in front of a beautiful, brand new house of at least 3,000 square feet. I found out later it had four bedrooms, a study, and three baths. Parked in the driveway was a new car in the $35,000-$40,000 range. As we drove into the driveway, you'll never guess who came walking out the front door. It was the young mother who just hours earlier had told me tearfully she would give anything to stay at home with her child. Here was a well-meaning and concerned Christian parent standing in front of a very large contradiction.

Dr. Bruce Shelley astutely comments: "Most Americans know that the steps toward the top are not easy, but they are convinced that the rewards of success are well worth the cost. So they shape their lives, public and private, to achieve their dream of the good life. The mother enters the work-force, infants enter day-care centers, and the whole family enters into debt."[5]

Let's paint a normal scenario for an American family. When a man and woman meet and decide to get married, it is not unusual for both to work. If they are college graduates and have master's degrees, they both pull down good salaries. Everything is fine for now. They have good incomes and they do not yet have children. But then she gets pregnant and now it's decision time. Who will care for this child?

Research indicates that among working women who become pregnant:

• Fifty percent are back in the labor force by the time their children are three months old.

• Approximately 75 percent of those women return to the same job that they had before.

• Seventy-two percent have returned to the labor force by the time their children are a year old.[6]

Half of these couples determine that the wife's part in providing income is so significant that she returns to work within ninety days of giving birth. Why is it so critical for the wife to get back to work as soon as possible? So the family can maintain the same level of income. As Philip Rieff commented, "A high standard of living . . . is considered the permitting condition for attaining a higher quality of life."[7] What a tragic miscalculation.

Nearly three out of every four women will be back on the job within a year. This is what I meant by the Second Industrial Revolution. And this one will prove even more devastating to the family than the first.

Once again, I pose the question: who is going to provide care for the children? It is clear from Scripture that God's choice for the privilege of caring for the child is the mother. Although this subject could easily fill an entire book, my remarks will be limited. As a matter of fact, my wife, Mary, *is* writing an entire book on this issue, so I will make my comments brief.

A number of couples have chosen to work and put their children in day care. But the evidence is overwhelming that day care is infinitely inferior to the care a child would get at home from mom. Here is a brief overview of recent findings from several research projects of day care in America:

• Day care during infancy is associated with "deviations" in the expected course of emotional development.

• Infants placed in twenty or more hours of day care per week avoid their mothers and are insecurely attached; sons have attachment problems with both mothers and fathers.

• Children placed in day care receive less adult attention, communicate less, receive and display less affection, are more aggressive, and are less responsive to adults.

• Compared with children who were cared for by their mothers as preschoolers, third-graders who were placed in day care as preschoolers are viewed more negatively by their peers, have lower academic grades, and demonstrate poorer study skills.

It is a dilemma for a couple to go from two full-time paychecks to just one. But the prospect of having children should be planned for and thought through in advance. A couple living on two paychecks should not get used to the lifestyle that comes with two paychecks if they want to have a family. Why not? Because someone is going to have to care for the family, and if both parents are working, where is the *quality* care going to come from? In my estimation, quality care does not come from someone being paid minimum wage to oversee a dozen two-year-olds.

Mother Theresa has treated a number of diseases at her mission in Calcutta, India. That's why her words are especially meaningful when she comments that "the biggest disease today is not leprosy or tuberculosis, but rather the feeling of being unwanted, uncared for, and deserted by everybody."

Historian John P. Koster documents some contemptible experiments that demonstrated the severe impact on a child who feels unwanted:

> It's a well known fact that children who receive an inadequate amount of love from their parents either die in infancy or grow up to be mentally and spiritually stunted adults. Stories about the absence of love are frequently found in literature beginning in the earliest days of history. In Herodotus, a Greek historian who wrote about 400 B.C., we find a narrative concerning Croesus, a fabulously rich king of Lydia, who performed an experiment in which he hoped to find out what the world's oldest language was. Croesus rounded up some unwanted babies, isolated them from all human contact, and had them suckled by female sheep until they learned to talk so that he could hear what language first came out of their mouths. According to Herodotus, though the children failed to thrive, they did survive, and they first uttered the word *bekos*. The king's courtiers couldn't agree whether this was an actual word or an imitation of the sheep.
>
> More than a thousand years later, according to a papal historian, the strange and mysterious German Emperor Frederick II decided to carry out the same experiment, but this time the infants all died before they were old enough to speak because they had been deprived of human affection expressed through the stroking and cooing of their nurses.[8]

God was obviously displeased at these coldhearted experiments perpetrated on such helpless infants. I believe that God is also displeased when Christian parents get sucked into the world's thinking and sacrifice the well-being of their children on the secular altar of self-fulfillment, career, and materialism. God has given us our children. And he intended for those children to be cared for.

By the way, do you know what all of the children in a day care center have in common? They all want their mommies.

I know a number of husbands and wives who are working hard to furnish both provision and care for their families. I know of one couple who finds it necessary for the wife to hold down a part-time job in order to make ends meet. They were able to work out an arrangement so that the wife could work three or four evenings a week. The husband gets home around 6:00 and the wife works from 7:00 to 11:00. But while she is helping to provide, he is caring for the children. This is an example of the husband helping with care and the wife helping to provide. But this does not negate the fact that he is to be the *primary* provider and she is to be the *primary* caregiver.

I know of another couple who for many years has made it a priority for the wife to be available to provide care for their children. They have purposefully adopted a lifestyle that is not as comfortable as some of their peers. They live in a small house in an older neighborhood, their two cars are sixteen and nine years old, and they are on a tight budget. Over the years, the wife has held a variety of part-time jobs. But guess who cared for their three kids in her absence?

If you were to walk into this home, you would not find a lot of new furniture, new carpet, or designer clothes. But let me tell you what you would find. You would find three very happy, well-adjusted, emotionally secure children who not only have been provided for, but cared for. And it shows. They will grow up to call their parents blessed for giving them the provision and the care that they so desperately needed and wanted.

FAMILY FUNDAMENTALS

We are talking fundamentals here, folks. One of the reasons that so many families in our culture are so stressed out is that we have forgotten the fundamentals. Frank Leahy, the legendary Notre Dame football coach, always stressed fundamentals. After an especially bad game, he walked into the locker room, held up a ball, and said, "Gentlemen, this is a football." The game of football requires a football. Other than that, it can be reduced to two things: blocking and tackling.

The fundamentals of football are blocking and tackling. The fundamentals of families are provision and care.

Please note that I am not advocating a return to "Ozzie and Harriett." Anti-family lobbying groups in Washington, D.C., often mock the biblical model of a family by calling it the "Ozzie and Harriet" family. I have a real problem with that.

As I recall that program, Harriet didn't work—but neither did Ozzie. Do you remember Ozzie ever coming in from the office? I don't think Ozzie had a job. All Ozzie ever did was go down to the soda fountain and get a quart of ice cream for David and Ricky. That is not God's plan. Men are to work, work hard, in order to provide for their families.

Someone needs to walk into our culture, point out the God-appointed roles for husbands and wives, and say, "America, this is a family. A family will need provision and a family will need care. God has ordained that the husband is primarily responsible to provide for the family while the wife is primarily to care for the family." Excuse me while I look for my bullet-proof vest.

Caring for a family has never been easy. No one said it would be. But the price we pay to follow God's plan is worth every cost. If you cannot make it on less than two full-time paychecks, and you have small children, then you may need to cut your lifestyle back to the point where mom can care for the children. That may entail some radical changes:

• Providing quality care for your children may mean moving to a smaller house.

• Providing quality care for your children may mean that you can't afford to buy nice furniture.

• Providing quality care for your children may mean that you can't take nice vacations.

• Providing quality care for your children may mean that you don't drive new cars.

• Providing quality care for your children may mean that you can't afford to buy new clothes for yourself as often as you'd like.

• Providing quality care for your children may mean that you don't go out to eat as often as you used to.

• Providing quality care for your children may mean that you become a card-carrying member of the middle class.

• Providing quality care for your children may mean that you will have to put up with such foolish inquiries such as "What's a smart woman like you doing at home?" or "What do you do all day long, anyway?" or "How soon are you planning on going back to work?"

Let me be up front here. If your children are in day care, why are they in day care? If you are a single mom and have to do the job of two parents and there is no other option open to you, then you should feel no guilt. You are doing the best you can and you are working to take care of the basic needs of your family. I am sure you are concerned that your children get the best care possible outside of what you could provide at home. You can find this type of care in a Christian day care center that views day care as a ministry to needy parents and an opportunity to meet the emotional needs of children. If you are in that situation, remember that God has said that he will be a father to the fatherless (Psalm 68:5).

I have met several dads who are raising their children by themselves. If God is a father to the fatherless, I don't think it's stretching it to believe that He will also be a mother to the motherless. In other words, He will help that dad provide the care that his children so desperately need. Whether you are a single parent dad or mom, *you are not alone*. He is there with you to help you cover all of the necessary bases for your children.

But if you are not in that situation, may I ask again: why are your children in day care? Is it possible that your thinking has been influenced by the world's perspective rather than God's? Is it possible that the real reason is that you have gotten used to a certain level of comfortable living? Is it possible that your children have taken a back seat to your career?

I have heard some women actually say that their children are better off in day care because they are being cared for by "professionals." First of all, the standards for workers in day care centers are notoriously low. Most centers have minimal education requirements; that is why they pay minimum wage. It is far from "professional." Second, there is no professional who can care for a child better than can the child's own mother. You may feel inadequate, but that doesn't mean you are inadequate. Through His Spirit God makes us adequate for any task to which He calls us, and your child will be thrilled to be with you instead of a "professional."

It is my goal in this chapter to challenge you to take any measures necessary to enable mom to care for the children at home. Gentlemen, some of you have been putting pressure on your wives to work so that the family can enjoy more income. I hope that you will be man enough to rethink what your family really needs. Your family needs quality care. And that means having mom at home. It will also yield a benefit to your marriage. It will give the two of you more time together. Wouldn't that be a nice change? When the husband provides for the family and the wife oversees its care, it's a win-win situation. That shouldn't surprise us; this has been God's ideal plan from day one.

The fact is that it's going to cost us something to provide quality care for our children. But they are worth it.

AMBITION IS THE KEY

What does it take to provide multi-dimensionally for our families? What does it take for a husband and wife to make a home a place of provision and care? The answer to both questions is the same. It takes ambition.

Not all ambition is bad! Selfish ambition is demonic, but that does not mean that ambition is wrong. Nothing worthwhile can be achieved without ambition.

What is ambition? Ambition is "the fuel of achievement."[9] "Like energy, ambition can be used for either good or destruction. It can burn cleanly, without odor, or burn in a manner that gives off noxious fumes. Like a flame it can become a runaway fire or the focused heat of the glassblower's torch."[10]

I like that. Ambition is the fuel of achievement. So it comes down to this: what do we want to achieve? Allow me to make four suggestions:

1. It should be our ambition to know God.

Thus says the Lord, "Let not a wise man boast of his wisdom, and let not the mighty man boast of his might, let not a rich man boast of his riches; but let him who boasts boast of this, that he understands and knows Me . . . " (Jeremiah 9:23-24).

More than a century ago, a young man stood before an audience and uttered these words:

The highest science, the loftiest speculation, the mightiest philosophy, which can ever engage the attention of a child of God, is the name, the nature, the person, the work, the doings, and the existence of the great God whom He calls His Father.

There is something *improving to the mind* in a contemplation of the Divinity. It is a subject so vast, that all our thoughts are lost in its immensity; so deep, that our pride is drowned in its infinity. Other subjects we can compass and grapple with; in them we feel a kind of self-content, and go our way with the thought, "Behold, I am wise."

But while the subject *humbles* the mind, it also *expands* it. He who often thinks of God will have a larger mind than the man who simply plods around this narrow globe. . . . The most excellent study for expanding the soul, is the science of Christ, and Him crucified, and the knowledge of the Godhead in the glorious Trinity. Nothing will so enlarge the intellect, nothing so magnify the whole soul of man, as a devout, earnest, continued investigation of the great subject of the Deity.

And whilst humbling and expanding, this subject is eminently consolatory. Oh, there is in contemplating Christ, a balm for every wound; in musing on the Father, there is a quietus for every grief; and in the influence of the Holy Ghost, there is a balsam for every sore. Would you lose your sorrows? Would you drown your cares? Then go, plunge yourself in the Godhead's deepest sea; be lost in His immensity; and you shall come forth as from a couch of rest, refreshed and invigorated. I know nothing which can so comfort the soul; so calm the swelling billows of sorrow and grief; so speak peace to the winds of trial, as a devout musing upon the subject of the Godhead. It is to that subject that I invite you this morning. . . .[11]

C. H. Spurgeon spoke those words when he was twenty years old. How old are you? Do you know God better today than you did a year ago? Than five years ago? Do you have an ambition to know God? There is a major difference between knowing God and knowing *about* God. It is a lofty and worthwhile ambition to know the God of the universe.

2. It should be our ambition to please God.

Therefore also we have as our ambition, whether at home or absent, to be pleasing to Him. For we must all appear before the judgment seat of Christ, that each one may be recompensed for his good deeds in the body, according to what he has done, whether good or bad (2 Corinthians 5:9-10, NASB).

It's a jungle out there and every day we must make decisions in the jungle. We make decisions about people, problems, schedules, ethics, and compromises. Some of these decisions are black and white but many of them are gray. How can we know what to do when a decision must be made on the spur of the moment?

The rule of thumb is this: what would please the Lord? There's your answer. It doesn't matter the circumstances, the situation, or the issue. The bottom line is always, does it please the Lord? That's an ambition that will get you through anything. If you are ever unsure of yourself, there is the solution. Make it your ambition to please the Lord.

3. It should be our ambition to give our careers to God.

Whatever you do, do your work heartily, as for the Lord rather than for men; knowing that from the Lord you will receive the reward of the inheritance. It is the Lord Christ whom you serve (Colossians 3:23-24, NASB).

When you go to work tomorrow, you might want to remind yourself for whom you are working. If you work at IBM, you do not work for IBM. It just issues your check. You work for Jesus Christ. If you work in sales, you don't work for your company. You work for Jesus Christ. If you are a mother with young children, you are changing diapers and carpooling for Jesus Christ. So change those diapers and make those sales calls to the glory of God.

Several weeks ago we noticed water marks in our family room ceiling. The tile in the upstairs shower had not been installed correctly and water was seeping through the cracks in the tile and leaking into the family room. The entire shower had to be disassembled so that the tile guy could come in and redo the job.

When he was done, another man came to reinstall the shower unit. As he got out his level to make sure the shower base was level, he asked me who did the tile. I told him his name and he replied, "If Tom put this in, I don't need to check it. That guy is the best tile man in town. If he repaired it, I'll guarantee you it's level." But he went ahead anyway, put down his level, and sure enough, it was level.

The next day, Tom the tile man returned to check the entire job. As he drove up, I noticed he had a bumper sticker that said "Praise the Lord." I asked if he was a Christian and he said he was. Then I told him about the compliment. Tom replied with an interesting story.

Four years ago, when he went to work for his company, his boss was concerned about the bottom line. He instructed his men to take any shortcuts in order to save time. Tom told him he wouldn't do that. If he was going to do the job, he was going to do it right. After several times of having to go back into a house and do the job over, Tom's boss began to instruct all of his guys to do their work like Tom. He realized it was cheaper in the long run to do a job correctly.

Tom told me he did his work for Jesus Christ. I smiled. I doubt we will have any more water coming through our ceiling. We found someone who installs tile to the glory of God.

4. It should be our ambition to provide and care for our families.

Both men and women in our culture are bombarded with the gospel of success. That used to be primarily true of men. Now women have joined the chase. "She's the ultimate woman—fit, trim, lively, independent, career minded. She's alone, no husband, no boyfriend, no children clinging to her," proclaims *Seventeen* magazine.[12]

In other words, the ultimate woman for the nineties is relationally malnourished. What a travesty when compared with God's plan! Over one hundred years ago, G. K. Chesterton asked: "Can anyone tell me two things more vital to the race than these; what man shall marry what woman, and what shall be the first things taught to their first child?"[13] Chesterton goes on to comment that

the . . . natural operation surrounded her with very young children, who require to be taught not so much anything but everything. Babies need not to be taught a trade, but to be introduced to a world. To put the matter shortly, a woman is generally shut up in a house with a human being at the time when he asks all the questions that there are, and some that there aren't. . . . Our race has thought it worth while to cast this burden on women in order to keep common-sense in the world. . . .

But when people begin to talk about this domestic duty as not merely difficult but trivial and dreary, I simply give up the question. For I cannot with the utmost energy of imagination conceive what they mean. . . . If drudgery only means dreadfully hard work, I admit the woman drudges in the home, as a man might drudge (at his work). . . . But if it means that the hard work is more heavy because it is trifling, colorless, and of small import to the soul, then I say give it up. . . .

How can it be an (important) career to tell other people's children about mathematics, and a small career to tell one's own children about the universe? . . . A woman's function is laborious . . . not because it is minute, but because it is gigantic. I will pity Mrs. Jones for the hugeness of her task; I will never pity her for its smallness.[14]

The responsibility of caring for a family is gigantic. That's why it can't be entrusted to other people. Children need to learn about life from their mothers. Children should have time to bake cookies with mom and to be free to ask questions about God as they spill flour on the floor.

Oswald Chambers once made an acute observation: "If we believe on Jesus Christ it is not what we gain but what He pours through us that counts. It is not that God makes us beautifully rounded grapes, but that He squeezes the sweetness out of us. We cannot measure our lives by spiritual success, but only by what God pours through us, and we cannot measure that at all."[15]

WHO MAKES THE BEST DISCIPLES?

A mother is a vessel God uses to pour Himself into children. A mother is a theologian, an educator, a psychologist, a counselor, an encourager, an embracer, a forgiver, a communicator, a listener, an explainer, a disciplinarian, a visionary, and a discipler. In my opinion, a mother is the best living example of what Jesus had in mind when he commanded us in the Great Commission to "make disciples."

Jesus was the great disciplemaker. If there is one word in this regard that occurs throughout the Gospels time and again, it is the word *with*. Mark 3:14 (NASB) says that "He appointed twelve, that they might be *with* Him. . . . " Jesus made disciples by being *with* his disciples. He did not pawn them off on someone else so that he could be free to go off and do something significant. In his mind, the most significant thing he could do was to be with his men.

He was with them when they asked foolish questions, he was with them when they ate their meals, he was with them when they went to the temple, he was with them when they went to the marketplace, he was with them just about every waking hour. He had to fight to get time to be by himself. Sounds like what a mother does, doesn't it?

Yet, Jesus didn't despise his task. He welcomed it. He made disciples each hour of every day. His men watched him as they were with him and learned subconscious lessons just from being in his presence. Sometimes, they didn't even realize what he meant by what he said or did until years later. And it was those *cared for* disciples who were *with* Jesus who changed the world.

That's the thing about moms. They have the ability to change the world right in their own homes. No wonder the enemy is trying so hard to get them to leave.

In 1908, Theodore Roosevelt said that "it is the tasks connected with the home that are the fundamental tasks of humanity. . . . After all, we can get along for the time being with an inferior quality of success in other lines, political or business, or of any such kind; because if there are failings in such matters we can make them good in the next generation; but if the mother does not do her duty, there will either be no next generation, or a next generation that is worse than none at all."[16]

What do you call a husband and wife who are both making sacrifices to give their family adequate provision and care? What do you call a man and woman who are ambitious to know God? What do you call a man and woman who are ambitious to please God? What do you call a husband and wife who rearrange their priorities and make financial sacrifices in order to build into the lives of their children?

You call them successful.

Why do you call them successful? I think the ultimate answer to that is beyond the realm of this earth. But one day in the future, they will stand before the Lord Jesus Christ. And when Christ looks at their lives and their choices and their priorities and their determination to provide and care for their children in a culture gone morally berserk, they will hear these words: "Well done, good and faithful servants."

Mark Twain once said that he could live for sixty days on a good compliment. Can you imagine the thrill of standing face to face, eye to eye, with the Savior of the World, and have him compliment you like that? Can you imagine the joy of hearing him say, "Well done"?

That is a compliment worth living for. And it won't last just sixty days. It will carry you through eternity.

Notes

1. Lee Eisenburg, "Watching The Clock," *Esquire*, April 1990, 43.

2. Patrick Reilly, "Publisher of *Sassy* wants to Dish *Dirt* to Teen-age Boys," *The Wall Street Journal*, 4 February 1991.

3. James Hurley, *Man and Woman in Biblical Perspective*, Grand Rapids: Zondervan, 1981, 32.

4. George Knight, "The Family and the Church," in *Recovering Biblical Manhood and Womanhood*, ed. John Piper and Wayne Grudem (Wheaton: Crossway Books, 1991), 348.

5. Bruce Shelley, *The Gospel and the American Dream* (Portland, Ore.: Multnomah Press, 1987), 122.

6. "Workplace," *The Wall Street Journal*, 6 February 1991.

7. Phillip Rieff, cited in Shelley, 119.

8. John P. Koster, *The Atheist Syndrome* (Nashville: Wolgemuth and Hyatt, 1989), 13.

9. Frederick C. Van Tatehove, *Ambition: Friend or Enemy* (Philadelphia: Westminster Press, 1984), 20.

10. Ibid., 21.

11. C. H. Spurgeon, quoted in J. I. Packer, *Knowing God* (Downers Grove, Ill.: InterVarsity Press, 1973), 13-14.

12. *Seventeen Magazine*, quoted in Terry Hershey, *Young Adult Ministry*, 39.

13. Robert Knille, *As I Was Saying: A Chesterton Reader* (Grand Rapids: Eerdmans, 1985), 141.

14. Ibid., 120.

15. Harry Verploegh, *Oswald Chambers: The Best From All His Books* (Nashville: Oliver Nelson, 1987), 342.

16. Theodore Roosevelt, quoted in *Digest of Family Trends*, Volume 5, Number 1, January 1991, 2

Part Two

*T*he Lord of the Jungle

Chapter 6

Federal Express or Pony Express?

If you refuse to be made straight when you are green,
you will not be made straight when you are dry.
African proverb

Reed Joseph was adopted as an infant into one of the wealthiest families in America. After graduating from an exclusive prep school in upstate New York, he headed west to play football at Stanford. After a tour of duty in Europe as a bomber pilot, he picked up an M.B.A at Harvard and a Ph.D. at Yale. Reed Joseph was a success. He was the last guy you'd think would be wanted for murder.

The following account is not a piece of carefully crafted fiction. It really happened.

In his early thirties, Reed decided to make a run at politics. He decided to go for broke and run for the United States Senate. He won. Reed Joseph was on a roll. Success just seemed to come his way.

Reed was considering his political future the night he and his wife attended the premiere of a new play on Broadway. Just for fun, they decided to take the subway back to their hotel, something they hadn't done in years. Little did Reed know that in a few moments his life would change forever.

As he ran to catch the train he heard screams. Turning to look, he saw an elderly, Hasidic Jew, wearing the traditional black suit and hat, being beaten by a man at least 6'6" and 300 pounds. The old man's face was gushing blood from savage blows. In a flash, the senator bolted toward the assailant and brought him down with the same force that had made him an all-American twenty years previously.

Quickly, the assailant was on his feet, charging him, a wicked-looking pipe in his hand. Sheer instinct from Reed's military days put the attacker on his back. With one blow to the throat, the man was in the fetal position, gasping for air. He never got it. Within seconds, he was dead—and so was the senator's career. Thirty-nine years old and he was finished.

As I said, this is a true story. It really happened. Except that his real name was not Reed Joseph. And he was not an American. And he didn't go to Stanford, fly bombers over Germany, or run for the Senate, and he never took the subway. Other than that, it's a true story.

So what's left? Well, he *was* adopted. They didn't name him Reed, but they could have, because they found him among some reeds along the river bank. They called him Moses.

His last name wasn't Joseph, but it could have been, for he was a descendant of Joseph, the great Israeli prime minister of Egypt. That's why his family was in Egypt.

F. B. Meyer gives some valuable historical information on Moses' life that is not commonly known:

> Moses was brought up in the palace, and he was treated as the grandson of Pharaoh. When he was old enough he was probably sent to be educated in the college which had grown up around the Temple of the Sun, and has been called "the Oxford of Ancient Egypt" . . . Stephen says: "Moses was learned in all the wisdom of the Egyptians" (Acts 7:22).
>
> But Moses was something more than a royal student: he was a statesman and a soldier. Stephen tells us that he was "mighty in words and deeds": mighty in words—there is the statesman; mighty in deeds—there is the soldier. [The Jewish historian] Josephus says that while he was still in his early manhood the Ethiopians invaded Egypt, routed the army sent against them, and threatened Memphis.
>
> In the panic the oracles were consulted, and on their recommendation Moses was entrusted with the command of the royal troops. He immediately took the field, surprised and defeated the enemy, and captured their principal city . . . and returned to Egypt laden with the spoils of victory.[1]

The facts of the story are this:

- Moses was adopted into the wealthiest family in Egypt.
- Moses was educated in "all the wisdom of the Egyptians." He went to the very best schools and had the equivalent of an M.B.A. and Ph.D.
- Moses was a highly decorated military leader.
- Moses, by virtue of his military leadership and his membership in the house of Pharaoh, was a logical choice to perhaps one day be Pharaoh (president) himself.
- Moses saw one of his Hebrew brothers being beaten by a taskmaster, went to his aid, and killed the guard.

The story of Moses is extremely contemporary. Many people today are devoting their lives to reaching the top of the pyramid. Moses was in line to *own* the pyramids. But Moses made a huge mistake that cost him everything. With one impulsive act, Moses fell off the pyramid. He was at the top, and one fatal mistake knocked him from his lofty position. His successful career was over, . . . or so he thought.

When we think of Moses, we tend to think of the plagues, the Red Sea, and all the other miraculous things God did for the children of Israel through him. But those events occurred in the last forty years of his life. We overlook the early years of his life. We cannot afford to do that, because studying his early years yields tremendous insight into how God often works in our own lives.

At about the age of forty, God called Moses to go back to school. Moses did not know this at the time. He thought he had completed all of his education. He had an Egyptian B.A., M.B.A., and Ph.D. But he lacked one degree. Moses needed an M.C.A. An M.C.A. is a Master's in Character Acquisition. For the role God had planned for Moses, getting that degree was mandatory.

The M.C.A. is not an easy degree. That's why so few sign up for it on their own. It usually takes a radical, unforeseen series of events to get people into the program—events like bankruptcy, divorce, moral failure, broken relationships, or a major career setback. The program consists of four core courses and a few electives (which God selects). It took Moses nearly forty years to complete.

The Master's of Character Acquisition is a tough program. Some of you may be in it and not realize it. But we are getting ahead of ourselves.

MOSES IN SCHOOL

Moses lived to be 120 years old. His life can be divided into three chapters of forty years each:

- The first forty years he was an unqualified success.
- The middle forty years he was an undisputed failure.
- The last forty years he became fit for the Master's use.

It is critical that we understand where Moses was in the first forty years. He was in the inner circle of the leadership of Egypt. Moses was the equivalent of a United States Senator, a member of the most exclusive club in the country. He was at the head of the pack—until he had to flee for his life.

Overnight, Moses went from being the greatest success story in Egypt to the greatest failure. No one knew it more than Moses. He knew in his heart of hearts that he was not in those privileged circumstances by chance. He was there for a reason. God had reached down and taken him from a family of slaves and placed him into the very family of Pharaoh. God had a purpose in mind for Moses.

Stephen gives us insight into what was going on in Moses' mind when he moved to defend his Jewish brother. Apparently, there was more at issue than just defending a helpless slave.

> And when he saw one of them being treated unjustly, he defended him and took vengeance for the oppressed by striking down the Egyptian. And he supposed that his brethren understood that God was granting them deliverance through him; but they did not understand (Acts 7:24-25, NASB).

Verse 25 makes it clear that around the age of forty, Moses knew he had been chosen by God to be the deliverer of Israel. He was right about his task, but he was forty years off on the timing. As a result, note what happened:

> And on the following day he appeared to them as they were fighting together, and he tried to reconcile them in peace, saying, "Men, you are brethren, why do you injure one another?" But the

one who was injuring his neighbor pushed him away, saying, "Who made you a ruler and a judge over us? You do not mean to kill me as you killed the Egyptian yesterday, do you?" And at this remark Moses fled, and became an alien in the land of Midian (Acts 7:26-29, NASB).

At about age forty, Moses instituted his own plan to bring about the Exodus. It didn't work.

This event gives us some clues about the kind of man Moses was. His goal was to take two million slave laborers out of Egypt and back to the land of their fathers. These people formed the economic backbone of Egypt. Yet, Moses believed that they would follow his leadership and revolt against Egypt and find their freedom. It takes a special kind of man to attempt to instigate this kind of rebellion.

He must have had great self-esteem.

He must have had great self-confidence.

He must have had great courage.

Moses believed in himself. He knew he was gifted and well-connected. He knew he had what it took to pull off the Exodus. Hadn't he succeeded in everything he had tried? That's why he fully expected to be successful in this venture as well.

He grew up in the first family of Egypt. He had the best of everything. He was groomed to be the best and as a result he had a tremendous amount of self-confidence and self-esteem. He had learned to rely on his instincts. Moses was a mover and shaker. He knew how to make a plan and make it happen. Moses was a leader with a capital L. Except this time. This time he hit a brick wall.

The account recorded in Exodus gives us another angle on the events that Stephen described. We must read this account carefully, because it gives us another clue into the personality of this dynamic leader.

> Now it came about in those days, when Moses had grown up, that he went out to his brethren, and looked on their hard labors; and he saw an Egyptian beating a Hebrew, one of his brethren. So he looked this way and that, and when he saw there was no one around, he struck down the Egyptian and hid him in the sand. . . . When Pharaoh heard of this matter, he tried to kill Moses. But Moses fled from the presence of Pharaoh and settled in the land of

Midian; and he sat down by a well (Exodus 2:11-12,15, NASB).

Notice one detail in the account. As Moses contemplated aiding his Hebrew brother, the Scripture says that "he looked this way and that." In other words, he looked around to his left and then to his right. But as several commentators have noted, he never looked up.

There is a type of self-confidence and self-esteem that is healthy and good. But there is an excessive self-confidence that is deadly to one's spiritual health. How do you tell the difference between the two? A wrong self-confidence is usually characterized by prayerlessness. We are so busy instituting our own plans and following our own instincts and are so confident everything will work as planned, that we never bother to look up. It's not that we are going against God; it's just that we don't sense we need Him. We think we can handle things without bothering the Lord.

In John 15:5 Jesus said, "I am the vine, you are the branches; he who abides in Me, and I in him, he bears much fruit; for apart from Me you can do nothing (NASB)." The person who has an excessive self-confidence doesn't believe that last phrase. He may believe it intellectually, but he doesn't believe it experientially. That's exactly where Moses was.

This is why Moses' failure tasted particularly bitter to him. He knew God had placed him in a position of power and authority to secure the release of the children of Israel. But he blew it. God had given him great influence and power specifically to rescue His people, and he failed miserably. It wasn't just his failure that depressed Moses; worse was that he was the only one on the horizon who could possibly help Israel. What other Hebrews were in positions of power or influence? He was it. Or rather, he used to be it. His golden opportunity and his people's one shot at freedom had vanished. What a tragic burden to carry for the rest of your life!

THE MIDIAN HILTON

Midlife is a time when many men undergo some type of transition. Midlife is when men are forced to come to grips with the changes in their lives. Consider the changes Moses faced at the age of forty.

Moses had a change of address.

He went from the palace of Pharaoh to the pastures of Midian. That's like going from the White House to running a gas station in the middle of the Mojave Desert. There were no Hiltons or Marriotts in Midian. It was God-forsaken territory.

Moses had a change of vocation.

Moses was a leader of men. Now he was a leader of sheep. Imagine the psychological and emotional trauma Moses suffered with such a drastic change in his life. This guy wasn't cut out to lead sheep. He was fit to lead a nation! But there he was, in the middle of a desert, governing a group of grazers.

Most men get their self-worth from what they do. Moses wasn't doing anything, except trying to find enough grass and water to keep his sheep alive. I think he must have suffered a tremendous identity crisis. In his own eyes, Moses was a failure, a failure with no hope of improving his circumstances.

Moses had a change of status.

Earlier in this book we talked about cultural success as an elevation in privilege, power and wealth. Moses had all of those things, then lost them. He didn't lose them gradually, but overnight. Moses experienced the original mid-life crisis. At about the age of forty, he went:

- from the palace to the pasture;
- from success to failure;
- from wealth to poverty;
- from significance to insignificance;
- from privilege to persecution;
- from freeman to felon;
- from a purpose in life to no purpose whatsoever;
- from a great future to a grim future.

Remember, all of this happened literally overnight. You've heard of an overnight success. Moses was an overnight failure. He lost it all in just twenty-four little hours. That's what you call a major league mid-life crisis.

All this convinces me that Moses must have struggled with

deep depression. Depression generally stems from some type of loss (unless the depression results from a chemical imbalance). Whether it is losing a spouse, losing a job, losing a sense of identity or self-worth, or whatever, the loss can bring depression. Moses lost everything. It doesn't make sense that he wouldn't be depressed. He was only human.

THE WORST HURT OF ALL

Perhaps the toughest change for Moses came in the emotional realm. His rejection by Pharaoh at least made some sense. But what about his own people? He couldn't understand why they had rejected him. It always hurts more when the rejection comes from inside your camp. It might be a friend, a loyal co-worker, a spouse or some other trusted person. That's why the wound is so deep. We thought they were on our team, but they rejected us.

At the outbreak of World War II, many Englishmen were so intimidated by Hitler that petitions were being circulated at Oxford and Cambridge urging Britain to surrender to Germany. Hitler was roving across Europe at will. His war machine seemed unstoppable. Most of Britain was defeated psychologically before the war ever started. But then Winston Churchill took charge as Prime Minister on May 10, 1940. In his first radio address of May 19, as France was collapsing under the Nazi onslaught, Churchill addressed the English people over the BBC:

> I speak to you for the first time as Prime Minister in a solemn hour for the life of our country, of our Empire, of our Allies, and above all of the cause of freedom. . . . Side by side . . . the British and French peoples have advanced to rescue not only Europe but mankind from the foulest and most soul-destroying tyranny which has ever darkened and stained the pages of history. Behind them, behind us—behind the armies of Britain and France—gather a group of shattered states and bludgeoned races: the Czechs, the Poles, the Norwegians, the Danes, the Dutch, the Belgians. Upon all of whom a long night of barbarism will descend unbroken even by a star of hope, unless we conquer, as conquer we must, as conquer we shall.[2]

One month later, leaders from around the world wondered whether Britain would quit if France were to be defeated. To answer this question, Churchill took to the radio again:

Upon this battle depends the survival of Christian civilization. Upon it depends our own British life, and the long continuity of our institutions and our Empire. . . . Hitler knows that he will have to break us on this island or lose the war. If we can stand up to him all Europe may be free and the life of the world may move forward into broad, sunlit uplands. But if we fail, then the whole world, including the United States, including all we have known and cared for, will sink into the abyss of a new Dark Age made more sinister, and perhaps more protracted, by the lights of perverted science. Let us therefore brace ourselves to our duties, and so bear ourselves that if the British Empire and its Commonwealth last for a thousand years, men will say: "This was their finest hour."[3]

By the power of his will and personality, Churchill "transformed cowards into brave men."[4] And the incredible began to happen. The British began to hope not only that they could survive, but triumph.

Five years later, those hopes were fulfilled. On May 7, 1945, Germany surrendered to the Allies. After leading Britain to victory against Nazi Germany, Winston Churchill earned his place in history. So how did the Brits show their thanks to the man who singlehandedly had turned them from an island of miserable cowards into a force of resolve and determination? On July 25, not quite three months after Germany's defeat, they displayed their gratitude by voting Churchill out of office.

Churchill was rejected by the very people he thought he could trust. He had pulled them together as a nation, and then with victory in hand, they turned on him.

When his wife told him that the defeat might be a blessing in disguise, Churchill responded: "If it is, then it is very effectively disguised."

That's how Moses felt. He could see no blessing in his circumstances. He could identify nothing positive about his new position in life. From a human perspective, he was right. No wonder he was wounded!

Moses was wounded, Churchill was wounded, and perhaps you are wounded. Maybe you have suffered some type of setback that has set you reeling. You may be feeling there is no recovery from your circumstances. But that is not true. The God who oversees and controls the events of history is overseeing your life as well. He knows exactly what he is doing. Perhaps you have lost control of your circumstances; he has not. Trust me, my friend. He has signed you up for a course which you didn't choose to take. If you remain teachable, he will ensure your graduation.

God was far from finished with Moses. Although Moses felt God had removed His hand from him, nothing was further from the truth. God's hand was as firmly on Moses in the desert as it had been when he was a babe in the bulrushes.

God had signed up Moses for a degree in character development. While he roamed over the desert for the next forty years, Moses took four core courses:

1. Unemployment 101
2. Advanced Obscurity
3. Remedial Waiting
4. Intermediate Loneliness

Let's look at each of these courses, because God still enrolls men and women in this curriculum.

COURSE ONE: UNEMPLOYMENT 101   .

Moses was a scholar, a statesman, and a soldier. Those kind of guys usually aren't looking in the classifieds for a job. With credentials like those the jobs usually come looking for *you*. When you have that kind of track record, it seems that every other call you get is from a headhunter, looking to see if you would be interested in a more lucrative position.

Moses had always been a success. Just think of his situation. Because of his position in Pharaoh's household, plus his academic and military accomplishments, it is safe to surmise that Moses was well off financially. He may have had a beautiful home near the country club overlooking a beautiful fairway. I imagine he could afford to go to Vail or Jackson Hole for a week or two to do a little skiing. He possibly leased a German-made chariot every three years or so. I assume his financial portfolio was impressive.

Let's put it this way: Moses probably didn't have to buy groceries with food stamps. Unless I miss my guess, this guy was set financially. And this is sheer speculation on my part, but do you think Moses may have had a touch of affluenza? It's hard to live in that kind of luxury and not have affluenza. Perhaps that's one reason God signed him up for an MCA.

It's hard for a guy like Moses to be unemployed. But that's exactly what he was. It probably took a week or two for the facts to hit him, but eventually he "got it": he was out of a job. This was no lateral move. It was a permanent setback with no chance of career recovery. It's easy for us to read this in the Bible and blow right by it. But let's not do that. This guy was stunned, hurt, wounded, embarrassed, humiliated, and probably for the first time in his life, he felt like a failure. Unemployment 101 is a tough course to take.

God still enrolls his men in Unemployment 101. In the last six months I have heard of two Christian executives, in cities two thousand miles apart, who have similar stories. These men are not acquainted with one another, but there is an amazing similarity to their circumstances. Each received an exceptional offer from another firm. They both talked with their superiors candidly about their futures. They both received assurances that they were safe from any cutbacks and were assured that they were valued and secure members of the team. They both turned down the job offers. And within six weeks, they both received their walking papers from the firms who were so "committed" to them.

Unemployment 101 inevitably attacks a man's self-worth. Most men get their self-worth from what they do, and Moses wasn't doing anything. I'm sure the two men I mentioned have both struggled over this issue. I know that I certainly struggled with it when I took Unemployment 101.

For nearly a year I was out of ministry. My time in Unemployment 101 came between my first and second pastorates. During that time I interviewed with seven churches and every one of them turned me down. I was thirty-two years old. I felt like a failure. Most churches don't want to hire a former pastor. They want to hire someone who is a current pastor. That's why eventually I had to call a guy for whom I used to drive a truck when I was in college. Fortunately, it was close to Christmas and he needed some extra help. So there I was, at the age of thirty-two, driving an air freight truck.

That was a very hard time in my life. I felt like a failure. I was hurting and I was wounded. That's what happens to most guys who take Unemployment 101. Quite frankly, it was a time of suffering for me. I think Moses suffered when he took this course and I think the two men I mentioned have suffered as well. Maybe you're suffering because you are currently enrolled in Unemployment 101. What causes suffering in Unemployment 101 is that you have no idea how long this course is going to last. In most courses, you know when the midterm and finals are coming. Then the class will be over. In Unemployment 101, the Professor does not hand out a syllabus announcing the important dates of the class. And that's the source of your suffering. "How long is this going to last?" you ask yourself time and time again.

Here's the good news about Unemployment 101. Unemployment 101 will cause you to suffer, but it's the suffering that qualifies you for ministry. But you may be thinking, *I'm not in full-time ministry!* You may have no desire to be in full-time ministry, but if you know Jesus Christ, you *are* in the ministry. Suffering will equip you for the unique ministry God has set aside specifically for you. He has not shelved you. He is simply retooling. And you are the tool.

COURSE TWO: ADVANCED OBSCURITY

Moses had gone from being somebody to being nobody. The rug had been pulled out from under him. Moses couldn't walk the streets of Egypt without being recognized. He never had to wait for a table in nice restaurant. People noticed him as he drove his chariot through the city. That's what makes me think Moses was not just confident, but overconfident. There is only one certain cure for overconfidence: obscurity.

Midian wasn't like Egypt. There were no cities or admiring groups of people. Midian was flat and barren, covered mostly by sand, rocks, and a few shrubs. It's a place of extreme heat in the day and extreme cold at night. It is rarely comfortable. That's why it is so obscure.

Moses didn't have a chariot and there weren't any restaurants or servants. When Moses fled from Egypt, he went to Midian and sat down by a well. Exodus picks up the account:

> Now the priest of Midian had seven daughters; and they came to draw water, and filled the troughs to water their father's flock. Then the shepherds came and drove them away, but Moses stood up and helped them, and watered their flock. When they came back to Reuel their father, he said, "Why have you come back so soon today?" So they said, "An Egyptian delivered us from the hand of the shepherds; and what is more, he even drew the water for us and watered the flock." And he said to his daughters, "Where is he then? Why is it that you have left the man behind? Invite him to have something to eat." And Moses was willing to dwell with the man, and he gave his daughter Zipporah to Moses. Then she gave birth to a son, and he named him Gershom, for he said, "I have been a sojourner in a foreign land" (Exodus 2:16-22, NASB).

It is important we understand that these six verses cover the entire middle forty years of Moses life. Forty years get six verses. Why? Because Moses was obscure. Not much was happening. There wasn't anything to report. It seemed as though God had forgotten about Moses, but He hadn't. In those forty years of obscurity, solitude and quietness, God was at work, rebuilding Moses from the inside out.

Could you be enrolled in God's course of Advanced Obscurity? In our frantic pace to get our piece of the American Dream, we don't take time to go back to school for a course like this. That's why God has to step in and change our circumstances. Some struggle with obscurity is required if you are going to earn your M.C.A. Obscurity is tough, especially if you are in a hurry to climb the corporate ladder. God doesn't much care about that; he wants you to climb the character ladder.

John Luther wrote that "good character is more to be praised than outstanding talent. Most talents are, to some extent, a gift. Good character, by contrast, is not given to us. We have to build it piece by piece, by thought, choice, courage and determination." There is no better place to begin making those right choices than in the circumstances of obscurity.

It may be an obscure job that is going nowhere fast. It may be a young mother with an M.B.A. who is taking care of two preschoolers instead of flying around the country closing deals. It may be an illness that came out of the blue which has put you out of your normal routine. God always has a deeper purpose when he enrolls his people in Advanced Obscurity. What is His purpose? You probably can't see it now; you'll have to wait. And if there's anything we hate to do, it's wait. Interestingly enough, that's why we He signs us up for the next course.

COURSE THREE: REMEDIAL WAITING

Moses was in a tremendous hurry to accomplish his task. Wasn't he nearly forty? If he was going to fulfill his appointed purpose, he needed to get with the program!

Peter Marshall once observed that "we are in such a hurry that we hate to miss one panel of a revolving door." I've got some bad news for you. You may be in hurry, but God is not.

We are in such a hurry that many of us cannot imagine our lives without Federal Express. "When it absolutely, positively, has to be there overnight." I don't know what I would do without Federal Express. I probably average one or two late-night visits a week to my local FedEx office.

What would we FedEx addicts have done one hundred years ago? Back then they didn't have Federal Express, they had Pony Express. I can see the commercials now: "Pony Express—When it absolutely, positively, has to be there in three months." Can you imagine waiting three months for a package? We have trouble waiting three days.

The bad news is this: God rarely uses Federal Express to build character. He doesn't overnight or fax character to us. It takes time to build character. Lots of time. That's why He is taking so much time in your life. God isn't in a hurry.

Can you believe God took forty years to build character into Moses? That's how long it took Moses to get his M.C.A. Most of us want character in forty minutes, and even then we're impatient.

I think God's motto is "When it absolutely, positively, has to be there in forty years." Moses was in a hurry to free the children of

Israel. He was sure God had placed him in his unique position so that he could have an unusual ministry. And he was right—but he was off on the timing.

God is not in a hurry when it comes to your life or mine. He will take all the time necessary to do a deep and lasting work in our lives. Because we're in a hurry, that seems very hard on us. Like Moses, we may even be in a hurry to do a good thing. But God is not in a hurry.

Did you ever see the movie *Starman?* The title character is an alien totally unaccustomed to earth. At one point, he begins to drive a car without any prior experience. When he almost causes a wreck and his earthling friend expresses doubt about his driving skills, he explains that he has been studying human drivers: "Red means stop. Green means go. Yellow means go very fast."

When was the last time you stopped when you saw a yellow light? Most of us accelerate when we come to yellow. Why? Yellow lights are indicators that we should prepare to stop. But we don't have time to stop. We are in a hurry.

That's why remedial waiting is such a difficult course for us. Yet it is absolutely necessary for the character God is building into our lives. Are you tired of waiting? You may be waiting for a promotion, you may be waiting to get pregnant, you may be waiting for your business to turn around, you may be waiting for employment, you may be waiting for your house to sell, you may be waiting for your child to finish those bone-marrow treatments, you may be waiting for that depression to finally leave.

May I offer a word of encouragement? You are right on schedule. Maybe not on your schedule, but on His schedule. He knows precisely what He is doing. Every trial has a beginning, a middle, and an end. You cannot determine where you are in your trial, but He knows exactly where you are. He is moving you along at just the right pace. Someone once said that everything is in walking distance, if you have enough time. We've got it.

You are not behind schedule, no matter what your feelings or other people are saying to you. Moses thought time would pass him by. Sarah thought she was too old to have a baby. Joseph wondered if he would ever get out of prison. David pondered when he would stop living in caves. If you are waiting, you are in good company.

Don't despair! As you work on your Master's in Character Acquisition, you've got plenty of time, because you belong to Jesus Christ. He literally has all the time in the world.

COURSE FOUR: INTERMEDIATE LONELINESS

Although Moses grew up in Pharaoh's palace, he was reared by his mother. God conveniently arranged for Pharaoh's daughter to hire Moses' mom as nanny. I think it's safe to surmise that Moses was not isolated from his family. Although he was a part of royalty, he was still able to enjoy contact with his mom, and I imagine to some degree with his father and his brother and sister. But on the day he had to flee for his life, those family ties were severed.

Loneliness is tough. It's tougher on us than most of us realize. Research has demonstrated that prolonged loneliness affects us physically:

- At Ohio State University College of Medicine, scientists found that patients who scored above the average in loneliness had significantly poorer functioning of their immune systems.

- In Sweden, a ten-year study of 150 middle-aged men found that social isolation was one of the best predictors of mortality.

- A report published in the journal *Science* said that social isolation is as significant to mortality rates as smoking, high blood pressure, high cholesterol, obesity, and lack of physical exercise. In fact, when age is adjusted for, social isolation is as great or   greater a mortality risk than smoking.

- At Stanford University School of Medicine, Dr. David Spiegel conducted research in which patients with metastatic breast cancer were randomly divided into two groups. One group received the usual medical care, while the other received the usual medical care plus weekly ninety-minute support group meetings for one year. Although he planned the study expecting that there would be no difference in life span between the two groups, five years later he found that the patients who attended the weekly group support meetings had twice the survival rate of the other group.[5]

Most leaders like to be with people. They enjoy the company of their followers. In the desert, Moses didn't have any followers (other than a few sheep). But Moses wasn't in the desert to lead, he was in the desert to be led. That's why he had to be isolated. God had to get him off by himself so that God could have his undivided attention. Moses thought he was a leader, but a leader really isn't a leader until he has learned to follow. God would not use Moses until Moses had learned to submit to God and to God's timetable. So Moses was alone.

In a period of twenty-four hours, Moses found himself isolated from every relationship he had ever enjoyed. He couldn't call anyone from a phone booth. It was over. No time for explanations, no opportunity to say goodbye. Moses was cut off overnight from every significant personal relationship he had enjoyed. Moses was alone. He was going back to get his Masters, and Intermediate Loneliness was one of the required courses.

When God calls us to take Intermediate Loneliness, he doesn't usually cut us off completely from all human relationships. Even though Moses had lost his family in Egypt, God gave him a wife in Midian, and before long he had two sons. But there was still a major void in Moses' life because of the relationships he had to leave behind.

William Manchester is writing a massive biography of Winston Churchill. He has finished two volumes and the third is in the works. The first volume covers Churchill's life from his birth in 1874 until 1932. It is a book of 973 pages—not surprising when you consider that it covers a period of fifty-eight years. Manchester's second volume covers just eight years of Churchill's life, from 1932 to 1940. You might expect that work to be significantly shorter. But this volume is 756 pages. It is roughly seven to eight times the length of the book you now hold in your hands. Interestingly, the title for the second volume is: *Alone, 1932-1940*.

In 1932, for the first time in his adult life, Churchill was out of public office. The consensus was that he was politically through. Churchill had been a legend in England for more than thirty years. In 1899, he was taken prisoner in the Boer War in South Africa but escaped,

> making his way across three hundred miles of enemy territory to freedom. His breakout made him a national figure. Returning home, he was elected to Parliament while Victoria still reigned. In the House of Commons his rise was meteoric. At thirty-three he was a cabinet minister. In 1911, he was named as the very first Lord of Admiralty . . .(later) he became secretary for war and air, and founded the Royal Air Force. Then, as colonial secretary, he was responsible for Britain's postwar (World War I) diplomacy in the Middle East. He planned the Jewish State, created the nations of Iraq and Jordan, and picked their rulers. Yet in 1931, Churchill had become a political pariah, out of joint with the times.[6]

The great man was now politically untouchable. He was alone—just like Moses. Loneliness is never pleasant. But God, in his wisdom, at times will separate us from our normal network of family and friends. Isolation is an opportunity to get to know God better. That wasn't true of Churchill, since he apparently did not have a personal relationship with Jesus Christ, but isolation did present that opportunity to Moses. It does the same for us.

THE BOTTOM LINE

So what's the point? Simply this: at this point in his life, Moses had to feel like an absolute failure. He had lost his career, his status, his reputation, his family, his friends, and his future. If that happened to you, wouldn't you feel like a failure? Anyone would after a string of experiences like that.

That's why some of you are struggling with failure right now. You have suffered some type of setback in your life and you struggle with failure nearly every waking moment. It could have been a career setback, a relational setback, or some other type of major loss. You are in the desert just as Moses was.

You probably aren't wandering around in the sand, looking for a Diet Pepsi. But you may be in a spiritual desert, an emotional desert, or a relational desert. You feel like a failure. You aren't. God has simply pulled you aside to enroll you in some courses for your character development. There is only one way to earn a Master's of Character Acquisition, and that is through hardship.

I like Miles Stanford's insight here: "Many believers are simply frantic over the fact of failure in their lives, and they will go to all lengths in trying to hide it, ignore it, or rationalize about it. And all the time they are resisting the main instrument in the Father's hand for conforming us to the image of His Son."[7]

Failure is not the end of things. Many times it's the necessary prelude to success.

When he was seven years old, his family was forced out of their home on a legal technicality, and he had to work to help support them.

At the age of nine, his mother died.

At twenty-two, he lost his job as a store clerk. He wanted to go to law school, but his education wasn't good enough.

At twenty-three, he went into debt to become the owner of a small store.

At twenty-six, his business partner died, leaving him a huge debt that took years to repay.

At twenty-eight, after courting a girl for four years, he asked her to marry him. She said no.

At thirty-seven, on his third try, he was elected to Congress, but two years later he was turned out of office.

At forty-one, his four-old-son died and it broke his heart.

At forty-five, he ran for the Senate and lost.

At forty-seven, he failed again, this time as the vice-presidential candidate.

At forty-nine, once more he ran for the Senate and lost.

At fifty-one, he was elected president of the United States. His name was Abraham Lincoln, a man many consider the greatest leader this country has ever had.[8]

Unless I miss my guess, I think Lincoln held a Master's of Character Acquisition. That's what made him such a great man. Lincoln was a man of character, unlike many of our latter day politicians revered by the public despite their sordid private escapades. Lincoln was a man of integrity and character.

Where did that character come from? It came from hardship and disappointment. For most of his life, Lincoln dealt with failure.

He was not considered a success. If you read his biography, it is clear Lincoln sat in on Advanced Obscurity, Remedial Waiting, and Intermediate Loneliness. He didn't simply take those courses, however; he passed them. He learned the lessons that could come only through hardship. If Lincoln had enjoyed meteoric success, his character would have lagged behind his achievements. So God allowed him to taste defeat, and it forged him into a vessel God could use.

Henry Ward Beecher wrote: "It is defeat that turns bone to flint, and gristle to muscle, and makes people invincible, and formed those heroic natures that are now in ascendancy in the world. Do not, then, be afraid of defeat. You are never so near to victory as when defeated in a good cause."

Everyone fails. But the true failure is the one who doesn't learn from his failure. That's why a teachable spirit is so important. When you are in the midst of a desert, the fastest way out is to ask God to let you learn everything He wants you to master in that experience. Stay open and stay teachable. God is not trying to ruin you, he is rebuilding you so that you can be used strategically. But God only uses people who have learned to be completely dependent upon Him. For many of us who are so self-sufficient and confident, that does not come easily.

Once Churchill got into an argument with one of his servants. "At the end of it, Churchill, his lower lip jutting, said: 'You were very rude to me, you know.' The servant, still seething, replied: 'Yes, but you were rude to me, too.' Churchill grumbled: 'Yes, but I am a great man.'"⁹

Churchill had an obvious flaw in character. He and Lincoln were miles apart in one respect. The difference between the two "great men" could not be more clearly seen than in an incident upon Lincoln's arrival in Richmond to view the city just captured by Northern troops.

> Admiral Porter, with an escort of ten seamen, took the President up the river and into Richmond. He says that on landing they saw some twelve Negroes digging with spades. The leader of them was an old man sixty years of age. He raised himself to an upright position, put his hands up to his eyes, then dropped the spade and sprang forward. . .

He fell upon his knees before the President and kissed his feet. The others followed his example, and in a minute Mr. Lincoln was surrounded by these people, who had treasured up the recollection of him caught from a photograph, and had looked to him for four years as one who was to lead them out of captivity.

Mr. Lincoln looked down at the poor creatures at his feet, and being embarrassed, said: "Don't kneel to me. That is not right. You must kneel to God only, and thank Him for the liberty you will hereafter enjoy. I am but God's humble instrument. . . ."[10]

Lincoln entertained large thoughts about God and small thoughts about himself. Humility means that someone has a proper self-confidence, a proper self-esteem, and a proper kind of godly courage. That kind of character only comes from being in the furnace of affliction and hardship. No wonder it was said that "the man Moses was very humble, more than any man who was on the face of the earth" (Numbers 12:3).

Do you feel like a failure? Then you are in good company. God is constantly taking people who fail and using them. Who else is he going to use? As John Gardner has pointed out, "there are not many undefeated people around."[11]

Our society is intoxicated with the idea of success. That's why we are so afraid of failure. But if you know Jesus Christ, your failure can be the back door of success, as Erwin Lutzer described it. God uses our failure to equip us for future success. That's what he did with Lincoln, what He did with Moses, and what He will do with you. When you look behind the scenes at some of the most successful people in history, you will find they were not unacquainted with failure. Failure became the bedrock that enabled them to handle later success.

God is still in the business of using people who fail. When you think about it, who else is he going to use?

Notes

1. F. B. Meyer, *Great Men of the Bible* (Grand Rapids: Zondervan, 1981), 157.

2. William Manchester, *The Last Lion, Winston Spencer Churchill* (New York: Little, Brown, 1988), 684.

3. Ibid., 686.

4. Ibid., 687.

5. Dr. David Spiegel, cited by Dr. Dean Ornish, *Program for Reversing Heart Disease* (New York: Random House, 1990), 91.

6. Manchester, xxiv.

7. Miles Sanford, *The Green Letters* (Grand Rapids: Zondervan, n.d.).

8. "To Illustrate," *Leadership*, Winter 1983, Vol. IV, No. 1, 83.

9. William Manchester, *The Last Lion*, 36.

10. G. Frederick Owen, *Abraham Lincoln, The Man and His Faith* (Wheaton: Tyndale, 1981), 195.

11. John Gardner, *On Leadership* (New York: Free Press, 1990), 113.

Chapter 7

HOW TO GET A PROMOTION

We last saw Moses in the middle of a midlife crisis. But as you know, God did not leave Moses in the wilderness. Moses was only in the desert to pick up an M.C.A. Once he graduated—and it took him forty years to complete his course work and write his thesis—then God started a new chapter in Moses' life. Moses was ready for a promotion. For the next forty years, Moses set a new standard for excellence in leadership. While he wasn't perfect, he had learned the lessons of the desert well. Israel enjoyed the benefits of his superb leadership for more than forty years.

But no leader leads forever. Some take early retirement, others lose their health. Some get fired, others keep showing up at the office until they die. Some leaders burn out prematurely. Others, like Moses, simply wear out. It took 120 years, but Moses finally wore out. For 120 years Moses was like Timex: he took a beating and kept on ticking. But eventually, even a Timex wears out.

Moses wore out at a critical time in the history of Israel. J. Oswald Sanders paints the scenario:

It is not difficult to picture the dismay and even despair that gripped the nation when the time drew near for the firm, capable hand of Moses to be withdrawn from the helm. For four decades their whole national life had revolved around him. It was to him that they had looked for solution of their problems and the settlement of their disputes. It was he who had interpreted the will of

God for them. They could be forgiven for feeling that he was irreplaceable. . . . The fact that his death occurred at the very moment they were about to enter Canaan imparted added acuteness to the crisis. They found it hard to believe that God had in reserve the very man to meet the crisis.[1]

But God always has his man waiting in the wings. People may wring their hands over a transition in leadership, but God never does. No matter how gifted a leader may have been, no matter how excellent his leadership, no matter how long he led, no leader is irreplaceable. People tend to forget that. A leader may be unique, but he is never irreplaceable.

Now it came about after the death of Moses the servant of the LORD that the LORD spoke to Joshua the son of Nun, Moses' servant, saying, "Moses My servant is dead; now therefore arise, cross this Jordan, you and all this people, to the land which I am giving to them, to the sons of Israel" (Joshua 1:1-2, NASB).

God had a man ready and waiting to replace the great Commander-in-Chief, Moses. His name was Joshua. At just the right moment, God promoted Joshua to the vacant position of leader of Israel.

Joshua's background was completely different from that of Moses. He never suffered a shattering experience at the age of forty that took him another forty years to get over, as did Moses. Still, Joshua did go through a wilderness period. And like Moses, his period in the desert also lasted forty years, although the two men's circumstances differed greatly.

Perhaps a good way to explain the difference is to imagine two men on separate elevators in the twin towers of the World Trade Center in New York City. The two men are Moses and Joshua. Moses occupies an elevator in the north tower while Joshua is in one in the south tower. Both get in their elevators on the ground floor and begin to rise over one hundred stories to the observation deck. From the observation deck they can look out to the Promised Land.

The ride is going along nicely, swift and smooth. Suddenly the cable in Moses' elevator snaps and instantaneously he plunges wildly to the basement. In a matter of seconds, Moses finds himself in the twisted wreckage of unfamiliar and unwelcome territory.

It will take him forty years to get free of the mangled and contorted circumstances of his life. The bottom had dropped out of his life.

Meanwhile, Joshua is in the other elevator in the south tower. He, too pushes the button to see the Promised Land. His ride up is unremarkable, but unexpectedly the elevator stops—no alarm, no jolt, no swaying, it simply comes to a halt between the fortieth and forty-first floor. Joshua is caught between floors. He is stuck. He will be there for forty years. Four decades will drag by before he manages to emerge from that stinking, confining box suspended hundreds of feet above the earth.

The bottom never did drop out for Joshua as it did for Moses. He just got stuck between floors. Or to put it another way, he plateaued. For forty years, he didn't go up and he didn't go down; he simply stayed where he was.

There's a big difference between plateauing and hitting the bottom. There is a big difference between a mid-life crisis and a mid-life plateau. The guy who bottoms out in mid-life leaves his wife and kids, buys a red Corvette and several feet of gold chains, and applies Rogaine to his bald spots three times a day.

The guy who plateaus in midlife doesn't do that. He still loves his wife and kids, he keeps his Olds Cutlass, the only chain he owns is in his backyard chain link fence, and spending money for Rogaine isn't on his budgetary priority list.

But whether the bottom drops out or life just plateaus, we need to see that both elevators are controlled by the same omnipotent and omniscient Operator, and each elevator contains its own lessons. Both Moses and Joshua were promoted by God to the top spot in Israel. But before they could be promoted, both were prepared. God prepared one by letting the bottom drop out; he prepared the other by letting him plateau.

CAREER PLATEAUING

Career plateauing is becoming a national phenomenon. A case could be made that it is the number one career dilemma in America. For years, many professionals expected to be promoted every two to three years. But things are changing. Promotions are coming along more like every five to seven years, if they come at all.

> Plateauing is a concept that says when a major aspect of life has stabilized, as it ultimately must, we may feel significantly dissatisfied. The essential source of the dissatisfaction is that the present is not engrossing and the future is not clear. There is not yet an answer to the question "What will I do next?" People who are plateauing are at a level, they are neither rising nor falling.[2]

That's tough when your entire mind-set is geared to climbing the ladder. When you are plateaued, you can't get it in gear. You are stuck in neutral. You're stuck between floors. And that's tough . . . especially if you are a driver. One reason it's so tough is because our expectations are so high.

> For a long time, history was on the side of the ambitious. From 1950 to 1975, we experienced an extraordinary period of economic expansion. American businesses dominated world markets, and it seemed that there were no limits to what we could achieve. During this period, organizations expanded hugely; governments, universities, hospitals, and other institutions doubled in size, and corporations increased by 56 percent. The major problem for organizations was finding enough qualified people to fill the managerial spots. . . .
>
> As a result, those who performed well were promoted unusually swiftly. People's primary goal soon became gaining promotion. If people worked in a large and complex organization, the possibilities for promotion seemed limitless when they looked up the hierarchical ladder. Increasingly, all rewards were tied to promotion, promotions were certainly possible, and *promotion became the only meaningful reward.*"[3]

For nearly a generation, promotion has been a gimme for hard workers. But the times, they are a changin'. Things today are almost the reverse of what they were. When executives with Ivy League M.B.A.s and fifteen years experience and six figure incomes are plateauing (and happy to still have a job), it doesn't take a genius to figure out that the promotions are going to be few and far between for everyone else on the corporate ladder.

In Search Of Plateauing

I never fail to be amazed at the number of books published on the subject of success. Countless books each year promise some "secret" that will ensure consistent promotion up the corporate ladder. These books are nothing new on the literary scene. More than sixty years ago, G. K. Chesterton wrote about the "success" books of his day.

> There has appeared in our time a particular class of books and arti-cles which I sincerely and solemnly think may be called the silliest ever known among men. They are much more wild than the wildest romances of chivalry and much more dull than the dullest religious tract. Moreover, the romances of chivalry were at least about chivalry; the religious tracts are about religion. But these things are about nothing; they are about what is called Success. . . .
>
> It is perfectly obvious that in any decent occupation (such as brick-laying or writing books) there are only two ways (in any special sense) of succeeding. One is by doing very good work, the other is by cheating. Both are much too simple to require any literary explanation.[4]

Chesterton is right. When you get down to it, good and con-sistent work is usually the right path to promotion. But in today's world even the workaholics are having trouble getting to the next rung on the corporate ladder. Some of them are willing to give up everything they have (including their families) to get to the next level.

Joshua may have been the very first guy to go through career plateauing. And what a plateau it was! It may have been the mother of all career plateauing. His career could be a case study in the *Harvard Business Review*. It may encourage you to know that Joshua finally got through his career plateau. Eventually he was promoted . . . but it was awhile between promotions. About forty years worth.

The story of Joshua fascinates me. It is chock full of principles that relate to my life and yours. In a world gone berserk with affluenza, looking at the life of Joshua will give us some clues about the significant things God wants to do in our lives. Let's begin by laying out three principles that rest on the solid founda-tion of Scripture.

Principle One: Ultimately, all promotion is from the Lord.

Principle Two: When God is ready to promote you, no person, no group, no superior, no human network can stand in His way.

Principle Three: God will test you before He promotes you.

It is customary to begin with principle one and proceed in numerical order. However, I would like to begin with principle three. Why? I'm not exactly sure. It may be that I'm tired and not thinking clearly. It may be there is latent rebellion in my life. Perhaps it's a carryover from going to college in the sixties. Or maybe it's the way I outlined this chapter. I think it's the latter. Anyway, let's begin with principle three.

God Will Test You Before He Promotes You

Moses did not start out as the leader of Israel. Neither did Joshua. That's because God's method is to test a man before he uses a man. It was true of Joseph, it was true of David, it was true of Daniel, and it was true of Paul. In God's administration, preparation always precedes promotion. God will teach the man and then he will test the man.

There is an age-old debate about leadership. Are leaders born or are leaders made? Well, every leader I have ever met had to be born. So yes, leaders are born. They *must* be born.

But are leaders made? When it comes to spiritual leadership, the answer is yes. God makes his leaders by *refining* them. God's leaders for ministry, business, home, academics, and everywhere else are refined through the process of testing.

God will test a person He desires to use in at least three ways. I mention these three because you find them so often in the lives of spiritual leaders throughout history. I think it is safe to say that almost any spiritual leader you can name has been through some form of these three tests. What is it that God tests? Primarily, it is a person's character.

Joshua did not come from an affluent background like Moses did. Yet Joshua would lead the people of Israel into a land of incredible affluence. It's easy to catch affluenza in that kind of environment. God was going to test Joshua to make sure his heart could withstand the allure of Promised Land affluenza. Without the right amount of tempering, affluenza could steal first place in Joshua's heart. That's why Joshua had to be tested.

Robert Clinton has pointed out a critical principle every leader and potential leader must know: *Character development comes before ministry.*[5] It doesn't matter if you are an accountant, a body and fender man, a professional athlete, a professor, a homemaker with small children, an entrepreneur, a pastor, an engineer, or a sales manager. God desires that all His people be His ministers right where they are. And you can count on this: he will test you before he will use you. Now let's look at three tests:

- The Test of Standing Alone
- The Test of Deep Disappointment
- The Test of Trusting God's Timing

THE TEST OF STANDING ALONE

Do the names Shammua, Shaphat, Igal, Palti, Gaddiel, Gaddi, Ammiel, Sethur, Nahbi, and Geuel ring a bell? If you guessed a law firm, you're wrong. Those names are not last names, they are first names. All these men had one thing in common: they were all chicken.

These ten were given an assignment, along with Caleb and Joshua. Moses ordered them to run a reconnaissance mission into Canaan to check out the territory.

When General Schwarzkopf gave his now-famous briefing at the end of the Gulf war, he briefly mentioned the special forces who went into Kuwait and Iraq to take a look at things before the land campaign began. They were the eyes and ears of Schwarzkopf behind enemy lines. That's exactly what Moses wanted these twelve guys to do. The episode is recorded in Numbers 13.

> When Moses sent them to spy out the land of Canaan, he said to them, "Go up there into the Negev; then go up into the hill country. And see what the land is like, and whether the people who live in it are strong or weak, whether they are few or many. And how is the land in which they live, is it good or bad? And how are the cities in which they live, are they like open camps or with fortifications? And how is the land, is it fat or lean? Are there trees in it or not? Make an effort then to get some of the fruit of the land." Now the time was the time of the first ripe grapes (Numbers 13:17-20, NASB).

This Israeli reconnaissance team went into Canaan to answer

Moses' questions. After forty days, they made their way back to Moses with their report.

> When they returned from spying out the land, at the end of forty days, they proceeded to come to Moses and Aaron . . . and they brought back word to them and to all the congregation and showed them the fruit of the land. Thus they told him, and said, "We went in to the land where you sent us; and it certainly does flow with milk and honey, and this is its fruit. Nevertheless, the people who live in the land are strong, and the cities are fortified and very large; and moreover, we saw the descendants of Anak there. Amalek is living in the land of the Negev and the Hittites and the Jebusites and the Amorites are living in the hill country, and the Canaanites are living by the sea and by the side of the Jordan (Numbers 13:25-29, NASB).

The report of the ten was at best pessimistic. They were like the guy who said, "I was going to read a book on positive thinking and then I thought, *what good would that do?*" Obviously, these guys had never read Norman Vincent Peale or Robert Schuller. But positive thinking wasn't the issue here. The issue was faith in God and what he had promised to do.

Caleb and Joshua were the lone voices of optimism, and they were optimistic because they believed in the power of God. But their ten comrades panicked. Caleb tried to get the floor but he barely finished a sentence before being interrupted by these ten jellyfish.

> But the men who had gone up with him said, "We are not able to go up against the people, for they are too strong for us." So they gave out to the sons of Israel a bad report of the land which they had spied out, saying, "The land through which we have gone, in spying it out, is a land that devours its inhabitants; and all the people whom we saw in it are men of great size. There also we saw the Nephilim (the sons of Anak are part of the Nephilim) and we became like grasshoppers in our own sight, and so we were in their sight" (Numbers 13:31-33).

These references to the sons of Anak and the Nephilim don't mean much to us, but they obviously meant a lot to the Israelites. The Anakites and the Nephilim were giants, people of tremendous size and strength. When the ten saw them, they felt like grasshoppers. That last line of verse 33 is significant. Because the ten felt like grasshoppers in their own hearts, that's exactly how they were perceived. They were beaten before they started.

Joshua and Caleb disagreed and took their stand against the weak and feeble report of the ten. But panic grew. Within minutes it had spread to the entire camp.

> Then all the congregation lifted up their voices and cried, and the people wept that night. And all the sons of Israel grumbled against Moses and Aaron; and the whole congregation said to them, "Would that we had died in the land of Egypt! Or would that we had died in this wilderness! And why is the LORD bringing us into this land, to fall by the sword? Our wives and our little ones will become plunder; would it not be better for us to return to Egypt?" So they said to another, "Let us appoint a leader and return to Egypt."
> Then Moses and Aaron fell on their faces in the presence of all the assembly of the congregation of the sons of Israel. And Joshua the son of Nun and Caleb the son of Jephunneh, of those who had spied out the land, tore their clothes; and they spoke to all the congregation of the sons of Israel, saying, "The land which we passed through to spy out is an exceedingly good land. If the LORD is pleased with us, then He will bring us into this land, and give it to us—a land which flows with milk and honey. Only do not rebel against the LORD; and do not fear the people of the land, for they shall be our prey. Their protection has been removed from them, and the LORD is with us; do not fear them."
> But all the congregation said to stone them with stones. . . (Numbers 14:1-3, 5-10, NASB).

This was Joshua's time of testing. He had to learn to stand alone. But wait. It's pretty clear that Joshua *and* Caleb stood against the ten. So Joshua really wasn't alone.

I would like to suggest that Joshua did stand alone. I would also like to suggest that Caleb stood alone. I think Joshua would have stood without Caleb and Caleb would have stood without Joshua. So in essence, both Joshua and Caleb stood alone. They just happened to stand alone together.

This was a heated situation. I've been in some pretty tense congregational meetings, but this one was a doozy. We should not underestimate the severity of the predicament. Joshua's life was on the line and so was Caleb's. Would they cave in to peer pressure? Or would they refuse to bow their knees to the idol of popularity? You know the answer. They stood on the truth and were not going to budge.

Why does God test this aspect of a man before God will use him? Because God's men must be willing to listen to God and to obey him regardless of how unpopular it may make them. God's men are not politicians who take a poll to determine what positions to take.

God's men must be different. They must lead from the power of their lives rather than out of a carefully crafted image designed by a public relations firm.

God's men stand for the truth when no one else will. Peter Marshall once prayed, "Dear Lord, give us clear vision that we may know where to stand and what to stand for, because unless we stand for something, we shall fall for anything."

God's men cannot strive for popularity. God's way is rarely popular. God is looking for people who can stand in the furnace and take the heat. You may be the only guy in your company who doesn't pad his expense account. If that is the case, you won't be popular. You will catch some heat. But the question is this: can you stand alone? Perhaps your boss insists that you lie in order to edge out the competition and close the deal. Can you stand alone and take the heat? Or do you cave into the affluenza that drives your boss to sell out?

May I ask you something? When was the last time you stood alone?

Standing alone is a process God uses to

• check your obedience
• check your integrity

When God calls a man to stand alone, he is checking a man's obedience in the midst of adversity and his integrity in the midst of a perverse generation. Some men pass the test. Others don't. It's the rare man in our society who passes. John Gardner comments:

> In recent years we have been puzzled by a steady parade of intelligent, successful Americans who have destroyed their own careers through amoral or criminal acts, from ambitious public servants to greedy Wall Street figures. Gifted and richly rewarded, they overreached and brought themselves crashing down. A common

assumption is that for a price (money, power, fame, sensual pleasure) they betrayed their standards. The other possibility is that they did not have any standards to betray, that they were among the many contemporary individuals who had roots in no set of values, or have torn loose from their roots. A society afflicted with the disintegration of family and community will inevitably feed such gifted transgressors into the stream of our national life.[6]

Reputation is what people think you are. Character is what you are when no one else is around. That's why God tests character. Moses passed this test and so did Joshua and Caleb. But Saul failed the test several times. In the clutch, Saul did not obey and he did not have integrity. That's why God couldn't use him. Saul always took the easy way out. If everyone else was doing it, he would too. If God wanted him to do something one way, Saul thought another way was better. Saul was a failure because he got into the habit of taking moral shortcuts. That's why he failed the test.

Charles Colson's words are appropriate here:

In my extensive travels over the past twelve years, I've met with pastors, talked with church members, and spoken in hundreds of churches. And from my observations I must conclude that the church, broadly speaking, has succumbed to many of the culture's enticements.

I don't want to generalize or be overly harsh, but it's fair to say that much of the church is caught up in the success mania of American society. Often more concerned with budgets and building programs than with the body of Christ, the church places more emphasis on growth than repentance. Suffering, sacrifice, and service has be preempted by success and self-fulfillment.

One pastor confided to me, "I try not to talk about subjects that make people uncomfortable. My job is to make sure they come back here week after week."[7]

Somewhere that pastor misread his biblical job description. His job is to please Christ and when necessary, to stand alone. That's it. Standing alone all comes down to who you're trying to please. Are you trying to please a congregation, a board, some powerful person in the denomination, an executive vice president in your company, or a well-connected person in your profession? Or are you trying to please Christ? You can't please both. And the only one who ultimately matters is Christ.

Are you a people-pleaser or a Christ-pleaser? That's the bottom line when it comes to standing alone.

THE TEST OF DEEP DISAPPOINTMENT

The ten spies miserably failed their test. Not only did they doubt the power of God, but they virtually incited a mob against the leaders God had chosen. The Lord was quick to respond:

> And the LORD spoke to Moses and Aaron, saying, "How long shall I bear with this evil congregation who are grumbling against Me? I have heard the complaints of the sons of Israel, which they are making against Me. Say to them, 'As I live,' says the LORD, 'just as you have spoken in My hearing, so I will surely do to you; your corpses shall fall in this wilderness, even all your numbered men, according to your complete number from twenty years old and upward, who have grumbled against Me. . . . Your children, however, whom you said would become a prey, I will bring them in, and they shall know the land which you have rejected.
>
> 'But as for you, your corpses shall fall in this wilderness. And your sons shall be shepherds for forty years in the wilderness, and they shall suffer for your unfaithfulness, until your corpses lie in the wilderness. . . .' " As for the men whom Moses sent to spy out the land and who returned and made all the congregation grumble against him by bringing out a bad report concerning the land, even those men who brought out the very bad report of the land died by a plague before the Lord. But Joshua the son of Nun and Caleb the son of Jephunneh remained alive out of those men who went to spy out the land (Numbers 14:26-29, 31-33, 36-38, NASB).

We never sin alone. Our sin always has consequences for others. When I sin, I must live with the consequences, but so must others. This is what happened to Joshua and Caleb. Though they had been faithful, they had to wait forty years to enter the Promised Land. That had to be a tremendously deep disappointment. It would have been one thing had they disobeyed, but they hadn't. They were obedient.

If God sets out to develop your character, at some point you will come face to face with deep disappointment. It will be deeper than you ever imagined. Why was Joshua plateaued between floors for forty years? Because of his sin? No, it was because of someone else's sin.

It would have been easy for Joshua to allow bitterness and resentment to get the best of him. He could have wallowed every day in a new pond of self-indulgent pity. That would have been the easy thing to do. But it would have soured his spirit and disqualified him from leadership. Every morning for forty years, Joshua woke up and had to make a decision. Would he live that day in bitterness or resentment, or would he trust God with his life?

Sportscaster Harry Kalas once introduced Philadelphia Phillies outfielder, Garry Maddox, with the following words: "Garry has turned his life around. He used to be depressed and miserable. Now he's miserable and depressed."[8]

How about you? Are you bitter and resentful? Or are you resentful and bitter? If anyone had a claim to either one it would be Joshua.

Perhaps you have been deeply disappointed by someone close to you. It may have been a brother, a trusted friend, or a spouse. Those are the deepest disappointments of all. Those kinds of broken trusts have more potential to open the twin poisons of bitterness and resentment than any other.

Leonard Holt was a paragon of respectability. He was a middle-aged, hard-working lab technician who worked at the same Pennsylvania paper mill for nineteen years. He was a Boy Scout leader, an affectionate father, a member of the local fire brigade, and a regular church attender, admired as a model in his community. Until the day he snapped.

On one carefully planned day, Leonard Holt, a proficient marksman, concealed two pistols in his coat pockets and drove to the mill where he had worked for so many years. Wordlessly, he walked slowly into his shop and began firing. He filled several co-workers with two or three bullets apiece, eventually firing more than thirty shots, killing men he had known for more than fifteen years. People were shocked. Leonard a murderer? It just didn't make sense.

Puzzled police investigators finally pieced together what lay behind this brief reign of terror. Down deep within Leonard's heart rumbled a mountain of resentment. His monk-like exterior concealed the seething hatred within. The investigation revealed that several victims had been promoted over Leonard. He was eaten alive by his bitterness and resentment and his rage finally came crashing to the surface. Beneath his picture in *Time* magazine, the caption told the story: "Responsible, Respectable, and Resentful."[9]

Leonard Holt was stuck between floors and it ate him alive. He allowed his disappointment to master him. William H. Walton once observed that "to carry a grudge is like being stung to death by one bee."

After the Civil War, Robert E. Lee visited the beautiful home of a wealthy Kentucky widow. After a charming lunch, she invited him to join her on the porch. She then pointed to a once majestic magnolia tree that had been badly burned and charred by Northern artillery fire. The woman began to cry as she described the former magnificence of the stately tree that had shaded the family house for generations. From her tears, she looked to General Lee for a word condemning the North or at least to sympathize with her loss. After pausing for several seconds, Lee said, "My dear madam, cut it down and forget it."

The only way to dispose of the deep roots of bitterness and disappointment is to redirect your focus to God. No one displayed how to do that better than Joseph, who said to his brothers long years after they had sold him to slave traders, "You meant evil against me, but God meant it for good to bring about this present result" (Genesis 50:20, NASB).

Joseph, in time, was able to see an explanation for the deep disappointment of his life. But long before he ever got an explanation, he had to remove the bitterness and resentment. So did Joshua. So did Caleb. And so do you.

THE TEST OF TRUSTING GOD'S TIMING

Just this afternoon I made plane reservations to take my family to Orlando. Mary and I will participate in the Christian Booksellers Convention and I am using my frequent flyer mileage to take the kids along. The majority of our expenses are covered so I thought we might as well take the opportunity to visit Disney

World. I was really pleased we could do this as a family, especially at such a savings.

But then I started to get less and less excited. As I thought about it, my enthusiasm dimmed considerably. Do you know what first brought me to my senses? This convention is in the middle of July. Do you know how many families will be in Orlando this July? My guess is half of all the families in America. In fact, I suspect half of all of the families in America will be at Disney World on the exact dates we will be there.

Then I began to think of the implications of being with 50 percent of the families in America at Disney World in July. Two of them will change my life.

First, we will pay large amounts of money to get into Disney World to do one thing. Do you know what it is? It's called waiting in line. Do you have any idea what it's like to stand in line for hours at Disney World in July? I figure if we get there early we can get on three rides in fourteen hours. The rest of the time we'll stand in line. Trust me. That is going to change my life.

Second, think of this: 95 degrees and 95 percent humidity. Standing in line at Disney World in July is like spending the day in the steam bath at the local health club. I can hardly wait. That will not only change my life, it will change my shirt.

What's funny is that this all started out sounding so wonderful. Now I'm not so sure. It seemed like a great idea. The problem is my timing. If we could have pulled this off the week before spring break, it would be a different story. The weather is great and all of the other kids are still in school. In three hours, we could get on fourteen rides. That's what I call timing.

God's timing is always impeccable. He never schedules something to come off in July that would be much better suited for March. His timing is always perfect.

We often have great difficulty in understanding God's timing. It doesn't make sense to us. From our perspective, He isn't even close to being on schedule. I'm sure Joshua had his struggles with God's timing. For forty years Joshua was plateaued in the wilderness between floors. Life was passing him by. God's timing can be enormously difficult to understand.

When Sally O'Malley of County Clare won the Irish Sweepstakes, she decided to treat herself to some of the finer things in life. "I've nivver had a milk bath," she told her milkman one morning. "Wouldja be bringin' me ninety-six quarts o' milk tomorrow?"

"Whattiver ye want, mum," answered the milkman. "Will that be pasteurized?"

"No," said she. "Up to me chest will do."

Sometimes it is extremely difficult to understand another person. It's that way in trying to understand God's timing. Rarely can you understand it in the middle of your circumstances; sometimes you won't even understand it afterwards. God tells us in Scripture that we will have a hard time with his methods. He tells us this up front, but we forget what He has said:

> "My thoughts are not your thoughts,
> Neither are your ways My ways," declares the LORD
> "For as the heavens are higher than the earth
> So are My ways higher than your ways,
> And My thoughts than your thoughts" (Isaiah 55:8,9, NASB).

When it comes to God's timing, we should not be surprised that His ways are not our ways. We should not be surprised that His thoughts do not line up with our thoughts. God thinks differently about timing than we do. His time is not our time.

I'm sure Joshua must have thought life was passing him by. Maybe you are having the same thoughts. But God's thoughts are not your thoughts. Your life is in His Hand. He knows precisely what He is doing with you. If you will be faithful, at the right time He will reward you.

Waiting for His timing is tough. You will struggle with it, and at other times you will fight it. But that's OK. It's part of the process as you learn to accept the control of the One whose thoughts are not your thoughts.

A young boy carried the cocoon of a moth into his house to watch the moth emerge. When the moth finally started to break out of his cocoon, the boy noticed how hard the moth had to struggle. The process was slow, exceeding slow. In an effort to help, the boy reached down and widened the opening of the cocoon. Soon the moth was out of its prison.

But as the boy watched, the wings remained shriveled. Something was wrong. What the boy had not realized was that the struggle to get out of the cocoon was essential for the development of the moth's muscle system. In a misguided effort to relieve the struggle, the boy had doomed the moth.[10]

God never allows the cocoon to open until the time is right. You may be feeling you will be plateaued forever. You may be discouraged because you have been stuck between floors longer than you thought possible. Don't lose heart! God is overseeing your struggle between floors. Remain open and teachable and at the right moment, He will do for you what He has done for so many others. He will provide a way of escape. And you will not only be free of your cocoon, but you will be fully developed and ready to fly.

Leonard Ravenhill tells about a group of tourists visiting a picturesque village. As they walked by an old man sitting beside a fence, one tourist asked in a patronizing way, "Were any great men born in this village?"

The old man replied, "Nope, only babies."[11]

There is no such thing as instant greatness or instant maturity. We have instant oatmeal, instant coffee, instant soup, and microwave popcorn. Some people just couldn't get by without a microwave. But in the Christian life, there are no microwaves. There are, however, crockpots. Crockpots are *slow* cookers. They need time, plenty of time. Spiritual maturity never comes in a package with microwave instructions. That's because spiritual maturity can only be produced in crockpots. God puts His leaders through the crockpot. Joshua was in the crockpot, Moses was in the crockpot, Caleb was in the crockpot, Joseph was in the crockpot, and you may be in the crockpot.

God puts His leaders in the very slowest of crockpots because when the time is right, they are not only done, they are tender. That's the kind of leader God can use. An effective spiritual leader needs a tender heart toward God. Tenderness can't happen in the microwave. It only happens in the crockpot.

Sometimes plateaued people wonder if God really loves them. They get so tired of waiting. May I let you in on a secret? God does love you. As a matter of fact, He loves you tender. And he will never let you go. Never. That's why you can trust His timing.

Our premise was this: God will test you before He promotes you. That simply means that God will work *in* you before He works *through* you. Then He can promote you.

A word of caution is in order. There is no blanket promise in Scripture that God *will* promote you. Some are promoted while others are not (*see* Hebrews 11:32-40). His blanket promise is that He will be faithful to you. And that is the most important thing. God will be faithful to do what is best for you. That's the promise of 2 Timothy 2:13, "If we are faithless, He remains faithful, for He cannot deny Himself."

EARNING YOUR STRIPES

We started with principle three instead of with one and two. There was a reason for that. Principles one and two go hand in hand.

Principle One: Ultimately, all promotion is from the Lord.

Principle Two: When God is ready to promote you, no person, no group, no superior, no human network can stand in His way.

Promotion cometh neither from the east, nor from the west, nor from the south. But God . . . putteth down one, and setteth up another (Psalm 75:6-7, KJV).

Psalm 75 is the ultimate statement about promotion. It is God who promotes. It is not your boss or your network or your office politics that promotes. God promotes. When He decides to promote it is a done deal. That's why we must be so careful to determine if God is behind the offer of a promotion.

Don't assume that a specific promotion opportunity is from the Lord. Check it out, pray it out, and talk it out with spiritually-minded family and friends. If God is in it, He'll give you assurance. If He's not, don't touch it with a ten-foot pole. Be willing to stay in the lower place, if necessary. When He's ready to move you on, you'll know in your heart. Until then, stay put. It's better to be plateaued in the will of God than to be promoted and be outside His will.

Don't get me wrong, it's tough to be plateaued. Mothers with young children can feel plateaued, men in mid-life can feel plateaued, single men and women can be plateaued in relationships with apparently no hope of fulfilling their internal desire to be married and have a family. Infertile couples who have been praying for years to have children can feel plateaued, single parents can feel plateaued when their lives seem to be going nowhere fast.

There are two options when you are plateaued. One is to yield yourself to the Master's wisdom and timing. The other is to bolt and begin scheming to get what you so desperately want. There is nothing wrong with changing your circumstances if you can legitimately do so. But if you can't legitimately change them, you can either trust or you can scheme. Warren Wiersbe is right: Faith is living without scheming. It is trusting God to love you tender and to never let you go.

He knows your situation. He knows your desire. And He knows the right time. In the meantime, be faithful where you are. Be as faithful as you can be and trust Him for your future. Remember it was the Lord Christ Himself who said, "He who is faithful in a very little thing will be faithful in much."

> "Father, where shall I work today?"
> And my love flowed warm and free.
> He pointed out a tiny spot and said,
> "Tend that place for me."
> I answered him quickly, "Oh, no! Not that!
> Why, no one would ever see,
> No matter how well my work was done;
> not that little place for me!"
> The word he spoke, then, wasn't stern;
> He answered me tenderly:
> "Nazareth was a little place,
> and so was Galilee."[12]

Notes

1. J. Oswald Sanders, source unknown.
2. Judith M. Bardwick, Ph.D., *The Plateauing Trap* (New York: Bantam, 1986), 3.

3. Ibid., 5.

4. G. K. Chesterton, *As I Was Saying* (Grand Rapids: Eerdmans, 1985), 68.

5. I am indebted to Robert Clinton for this succinct statement. See J. Robert Clinton, *The Making of a Leader* (Colorado Springs, Colo.: NavPress, 1988).

6. John Gardner, *On Leadership* (New York: The Free Press, 1990), 114.

7. Charles Colson, *Against the Night* (Ann Arbor: Servant, 1989), 103.

8. Michael Green, *Illustrations for Biblical Preaching* (Grand Rapids: Baker, 1989), 326.

9. Ibid., 302.

10. Ibid., 384.

11. Leonard Ravenhill, *Leadership*, Spring Quarter, 1984, 45.

12. Cited by David Roper, *The Strength of a Man* (Grand Rapids: Discovery House, 1989), 110.

Chapter 8

JUNGLE LAMBCHOPS

I am the good shepherd;
and I know My own, and My own know Me.
Jesus Christ (John 10:14)

Sheep don't fit in the jungle. Lions, they fit. Tigers, they fit. Elephants, gorillas, and parrots, they all fit. But sheep don't fit. They are out of place in the jungle. It's just not their turf. In the jungle, a sheep could easily be transformed into lambchops within seconds. That's why sheep normally don't hang out in the jungle.

Close to two hundred times in Scripture God's people are called sheep. Just think of the magnitude of creation. He could have called us eagles, gorillas, collies, or armadillos. But He didn't. He calls us sheep.

Psalm 23 is a dangerous section of the Bible. It is dangerous because we know it so well. Many of us have memorized Psalm 23. Even many non-Christians know Psalm 23. The danger of Psalm 23 is that we are so familiar with it that it has lost its significance.

Psalm 23 has something special for those of us raising families in a fast track society. Psalm 23 speaks to the pressures of our culture. It is remarkably contemporary. Psalm 23 is critical because it ultimately tells us how to survive in the jungle. Psalm 23 is a survival manual for the modern day jungle. It tells us how to be *in* the jungle, but not *of* the jungle. Every sheep needs to know it well. It will keep you from the lambchop experience every sheep wants to avoid.

The Lord is my shepherd,
  I shall not want.
He makes me lie down in green pastures;
He leads me beside quiet waters.
 He restores my soul;
He guides me in the paths of righteousness
  for His name's sake.
Even though I walk through the valley of the shadow of
  death,
I fear no evil; for Thou art with me;
  Thy rod and Thy staff, they comfort me.
Thou dost prepare a table before me in the presence of my
  enemies;
Thou hast anointed my head with oil;
  My cup overflows.
Surely goodness and mercy will follow me all the days of my
  life,
And I will dwell in the house of the LORD forever.

I didn't grow up on a farm. I grew up in new subdivisions with new streets and new houses. My dad built and sold new houses. So there weren't any sheep in our neighborhood. As a result, I knew next to nothing about sheep. So I decided to do some research on sheep. I discovered three things about sheep that intrigued me.

First, I learned that *sheep are stupid.* Every couple of years or so, I take my family to the Barnum and Bailey Ringling Brothers Circus. It's the greatest show on earth. Over the years, we have seen trained lions, trained elephants, trained horses, and even trained poodles. But we have never seen trained sheep. There's one explanation for that: sheep are stupid.

Two hundred times in Scripture God calls us sheep. I'll let you make whatever personal application from that you want to. I don't know about you, but the principle of stupidity certainly fits in my life. That's why I need a shepherd. I'm a sheep and I'm stupid.

The second thing I learned about sheep is this: *sheep are dirty.* Growing up in the city, I had always thought that pigs were dirty, but much to my surprise, I discovered that sheep are far dirtier than pigs.

At our house we have a little cat named Emily. Emily is forever licking her little paws and cleaning herself. Many animals are careful to keep themselves clean. Not sheep. Sheep are dirty animals who need someone to keep them clean. That's why sheep need a shepherd. That's why God calls us sheep. We need a Shepherd to keep us clean.

Third, I learned that *sheep are defenseless*. Most animals have some type of defense mechanism to protect them from assailants. But not sheep. Sheep are defenseless. There have actually been incidents of raven or crows flying down on a sheep's head and plucking out the sheep's eyes. Sheep have no way of defending themselves against such attack. They can't bark, they can't emit a noxious odor, they can't use their claws because they don't have claws. Sheep are defenseless.

I enjoy football. Every football team picks out a suitable name for itself. Whether it's high school, college, or pro, a team must have an appropriate label for its team. Generally speaking, football teams pick their names from one of two categories. Football teams are usually named after groups of fighting men or some type of animal.

All football fans know about the San Francisco 49ers, but few fans outside of California have any idea what the term '49er' means. In 1849, gold was discovered in California at Sutter's Mill. A gold rush quickly ensued, and men from all over the world came to the foothills of the Sierras to make their fortune. These tough, aggressive risk-takers were known as 49ers. The 49ers were a group of fighting men.

The other category football teams fall into are teams that take their names from animals. Teams like the Chicago Bears and Detroit Lions. Some teams get exotic, like the University of California-Irvine Anteaters. Almost every animal has been adopted by some team as their mascot. But I have never heard of the New Orleans Sheep or the Boston Sheep. Teams aren't named after sheep, because sheep are defenseless.

Someone is thinking, *what about the Los Angeles Rams?* That's a different kind of sheep, and they are not defenseless. God didn't call us rams, he called us sheep. There's not a football team on this planet that wants to be called sheep. Yet that's what God calls us. We are defenseless. That's why we need a shepherd.

A SHEEPISH LOOK AT PSALM 23

It is easy to overlook that Psalm 23 is written from the perspective of the sheep. That is critical to understand. Imagine yourself as a sheep (since you are a sheep) resting comfortably on a green, rolling hillside in Palestine. There is plenty of water and plenty of grass. As you repose on the hillside, you look out about seventy-five yards away where your Shepherd is standing guard over the flock. Psalm 23 is written from this perspective. The sheep is looking at his shepherd and describing what his shepherd is like. So mentally, we need to get down on all fours to get into the fabric and texture of this Psalm.

The theme of the Psalm is found in verse 1:

> The Lord is my shepherd,
> I shall not want.

Everyone has a shepherd. For some, the shepherd is money, for others it is success. For some it is making it to the top of the corporate ladder, for others it is social status and being with the right people. Everyone has a shepherd, a master, a ruler.

This little sheep says that the Lord is *my* shepherd. Not everyone can say that. In our culture, many people know *about* the shepherd, but they don't *know* the shepherd. There is a difference between knowing about someone and knowing him. Pastor John MacArthur tells of a man who recently came into his office who was looking for a shepherd:

> Not long ago a man I had never met before walked into my office and said, "I need help. I feel strange coming to you, because I'm not even a Christian. I'm Jewish. Until a few weeks ago I had never even been in a church. But I need help from someone, so I decided to talk to you.
>
> "I've been divorced twice, and now I'm living with a woman who is my lover. I don't even like her, but I haven't got the courage to leave her and go back to my second wife.
>
> "I'm a medical doctor. Worse, I'm an abortionist. I kill babies for a living. Last year in my clinic we did nine million dollars' worth of abortions. I don't do therapeutic abortions; I do abortions for any

reason. And if a woman doesn't have a reason, I give her a reason.

"Six weeks ago I came to Grace Community Church on a Sunday morning, and I've been coming every week since. Last week you preached a message called 'Delivered to Satan.' If there was ever anyone on earth who was delivered to Satan, it's me. I know I'm doomed to hell because of what I've done. I'm absolutely unhappy. I'm continually seeing a psychoanalyst and I'm not getting any help at all. I can't stand the guilt of this. I don't know what to do about it. Can you help me?"

I said to him, "No, I can't help you."

He looked at me, startled. Sheer desperation was in his face.

I let it sink in.

Then I said, "But I know someone who can help you: Jesus Christ."

He said sadly, "But I don't know who He is. I've been taught all my life not to believe in Him."

I said, "Would you like to know who Jesus Christ is?"

He said, "I would if He can help me."

MacArthur then did something unusual. He gave the man a Bible and showed him the Gospel of John. He then told the man to go home and read the Gospel until he knew who Jesus Christ was. He told the man to call him when he knew who Jesus Christ was. Within a week or so, the man was back in his office.

"I know who He is."

I said, "You do?"

He said, "Yes, I do."

"Who is He?" I asked.

"I'll tell you one thing, He's not just a man."

I said, "Really, who is he?"

"He's God!" he said with finality.

"You, a Jew, are telling me that Jesus Christ is God?" I asked. "How do you know that?"

He said, "It's clear. It's right there in the Gospel of John."

"What convinced you?" I asked.

"Look at the words He said, and look at the things He did! No one could say and do those things unless He was God." He was echoing the apostle John's thesis perfectly.

I nodded enthusiastically.

He was on a roll. "Do you know what else He did? He rose from the dead! They buried Him, and three days later, He came back from the dead! That proves He is God, doesn't it? God himself came into this world!"

I asked him, "Do you know why He came?"

"Yes. He came to die for my sin."

"How do you know that?" I asked.

"Because I liked John so well I read Romans. And as soon as I clean up my life I'm going to become a Christian."

I said, "That's the wrong approach. Receive him as your Lord and Savior now, and let Him clean up your life." Then I asked the man, "What would such a decision mean in your career?"

"Well," he said, "I spent this afternoon writing my resignation letter to the abortion clinic. When I get out of here I'm going to call my second wife and bring her to church with me." And he did.[1]

That doctor can now say, "The Lord is *my* shepherd." What was his shepherd before that? Nine million bucks a year. That's affluenza. It's also child sacrifice. But Christ became his shepherd and all of that dirt has been washed away by the sacrifice of the Good Shepherd.

In John 10:27, Jesus said, "My sheep hear my voice, and I know them, and they follow me. . . ."

In Israel, when David was writing Psalm 23, sheep from various flocks frequently fed in the same area. Hundreds and even thousands of sheep intermingled as they grazed. Since there was little walled or fenced pastureland, how could the shepherds identify their own sheep?

It's amazing how simple the solution was. When a shepherd was ready to move on, he would simply call out to his sheep. That was all he had to do. His sheep knew *his* voice and they would follow him. And the other sheep would stay put because they had not heard the voice of their shepherd.

How do we hear the voice of our shepherd today? He definitely speaks to us. Different people will make incredible claims about God speaking to them. Some of them hear audible voices, some of them have visions. Personally, the only time I have a vision is when I eat Mexican food after 9 P.M.

Yet, God does speak to us today. He speaks to us just like he spoke to that Jewish doctor. God speaks to us in His Word. That's where we can be assured of hearing His voice. There are a lot of voices out there. But His direction and will for every circumstance of life is outlined in Scripture. That's how the Holy Spirit will lead us.

The sheep not only hear the Shepherd's voice, they follow the Shepherd's voice. All of the sheep from various flocks would hear the voice of the one shepherd who was calling out, but only his sheep would hear his voice and follow him. What's the most important voice in your life? Is it your desire to follow Him? Then you are one of His sheep. And you can be assured that you will make it through the jungle.

Jesus said, "My sheep hear My voice, and I know them, and they follow Me; and I give eternal life to them, and they shall never perish; and no one shall snatch them out of My hand" (John 10:27-28, NASB). That's why you'll make it through the jungle. The Lord is your shepherd. It doesn't matter what may come in life. You are in His hands. You are safe. And you are secure.

When David says "the Lord is my shepherd, I shall not want," he means that if the Lord is your shepherd, *every* area and activity of your life is under His direction, His protection, and His control. Every other verse in Psalm 23 underscores this fact.

THE SHEPHERD PROVIDES REST IN THE JUNGLE

I have three children and over the years I have noticed something about them. They have never, ever been tired. Their eyes may sag, their speech may slur, their legs may give way, but if I say, "Josh, are you tired?" he will immediately say, "No." So will Rachel and John.

My kids have never been tired in history. Let's put it another way. Kids will never admit to being tired. Because if they admit that they are tired, you may have them take a nap. And there is nothing worse to a kid than a nap. Kids hate naps. Their parents would kill to get a nap, but kids hate them. It's funny how that works. Kids are never tired, but their parents are exhausted.

Sheep are like kids. They won't admit when they are tired. That's why verse 2 says: "He makes me lie down in green pastures."

When my kids were small, I used to take them upstairs and put them down for a nap in their crib. I particularly remember putting Josh down for a nap one afternoon. He was exceptionally tired and cranky, since we had been at church longer than usual that morning. Then we went out to lunch. By the time we got home, he was at the end of his rope.

I put him down in the crib, walked out, and shut the door. I stood by the door for a minute to make sure he was going to be still. Within ten seconds of shutting the door, I heard him grunting and puffing as he pulled himself up on the railing of the crib. I opened the door to see him peering over the side of the crib at me. Josh didn't want to take a nap. He mumbled in baby talk, "No nap, Dada."

I put him back down on the mattress, and this time I put my hand on his little back. He didn't like that, and he tried to get up again. So I put a little bit more pressure on his back. He still wanted to get up, but I wouldn't lift my hand. He tried to get up a few more times but could never quite muster enough strength to get beyond my hand. Within minutes, he gave up and went to sleep. Josh didn't want to go sleep, although he desperately needed to rest. So I had to *make* him lie down.

That's what the Shepherd has to do with us sometimes. He *makes* us lie down. We get busy, overcommitted, caught up in the rat race. So he will make us lie down. He will use some event or some circumstance to make us lie down. He can use a financial setback to make us lie down. He can use a heart attack to make us lie down. He can use a job layoff to make us lie down.

Some of you may have problems with that. You've been told it is always God's will for you to be prosperous and healthy. That is simply not the case. God is much more concerned about your spiritual health than he is about your physical or financial health. He will even choose at times to deny us physical health in order to bring about spiritual rest. We will resist him like a little child resisting the hand of his father. But the Shepherd knows what's best. He will make you lie down.

But don't forget this—He makes us lie down in green pastures. "Aha!" someone is saying. "Those pastures are green! He doesn't make us lie down in brown pastures. It is God's will that we always be healthy and prosperous! The green pastures signify health and prosperity!"

The reason he has to *make* sheep lie down in green pastures is that sheep don't always realize the pastures are green. Sheep have a tendency to think the grass is always greener on the other side of the hill. I don't know about you, but I have a tendency to be color-blind. Color-blind spiritually, that is. God has made me lie down in some pastures that sure didn't look green to me. In fact, they looked very brown. I checked with some other sheep and they also thought the pastures were brown. That's why I didn't want to lie down. It wasn't green enough for me.

There are many shades of green in the Christian life and one of them is brown. Your pasture may not look green right now. All you can see is brown. No wonder you don't want to lie down.

That happened to me a number of years ago when I took Unemployment 101. One day God decided I would be better off without a job. Suddenly everything I touched turned to brown. We went through our savings, then had to sell our second car just to make it for another month or two. Then the car money ran out. During this time, Mary had two surgeries and I got meningitis.

Finally, we found out Mary was pregnant with Josh. Because of the medicine she had been taking to break down a blood clot lodged in her abdomen, a doctor told Mary we would probably have a deformed child. All of the above events transpired in less than ten months. That's not what I call green pastures. At the time, those pastures looked very brown indeed.

The pastures were so brown that for the first time I struggled with depression. I went through a tunnel that took me two years to get through. I like to have fun and laugh as much as the next guy, but for two years the only time I laughed was when I would play with my kids and they would do or say something cute. Other than that, I didn't laugh. There was nothing to laugh about.

During that time, God was working on my character. I could not understand why everything I touched turned to brown. Nothing was working in my life. I felt like a quarterback who took the snap from center, dropped back to pass, and was sacked by his own offensive line. I wanted to remind God that I was on his team. My name was in his program. My jersey was the right color. But I felt He was against me.

He wasn't against me, he was just rebuilding me. He was teaching me some difficult lessons in the short-term so I might be more effective in the long term. He was teaching me sympathy for those who hurt by allowing me to hurt. Up to then, that had been a dimension seriously lacking in my life. He was teaching me not to be so confident in myself, but to be confident in Him. It was necessary for Him to allow all my carefully laid plans to fall apart in such a rubble that they could never be repaired. Then He stepped in and put everything back together.

At the time I saw nothing but brown pastures. It was a time of spiritual drought in my life. I was angry at God and I resented what He was doing to me. But as the time has gone by, I look back on those days and can see nothing but green pastures.

God was so faithful to me. He determined to make some needed repairs in my heart and character before it was too late. I didn't realize what He was doing. I didn't realize I was in surgery. God was operating on me spiritually just as a surgeon would operate on me physically. I had some malignant tumors of selfishness and arrogance that had to be removed. God loved me enough to operate. That's why there was pain and discomfort. But as I look back on that difficult time, I can see the good hand of the Shepherd. When the Shepherd is in control of your life, even the brown pastures become green.

If you are looking around at the circumstances of your life and all you see is brown, don't lose heart. Perhaps your business has failed, perhaps you are reading this in a hospital room, perhaps you are in the middle of another round of chemotherapy, perhaps a cohort at work has just pulled off a political scheme and has edged you out of a well-deserved promotion. Maybe you feel God has put you on permanent hold. Maybe you feel He has abandoned you.

Trust the Shepherd, my friend. You cannot see it now, but you are plateaued in green pastures that look brown. Remain open and teachable. Pray that you will learn everything He has for you in this situation. Keep a teachable spirit. One day you will look back to when He made you lie down and you'll say, "You know, those pastures really were green."

If He has pulled you out of the mainstream of life, it's only because He knows you need the rest. You may also need surgery, and the only way to get over surgery is to rest quietly. You can afford to do that. Submit to that firm, loving hand on your back. When you have rested sufficiently, He will let you get back up.

THE SHEPHERD PROVIDES REFRESHMENT IN THE JUNGLE

A shepherd is a leader. Verse 2 says:

He *leads* me beside quiet waters.

There are two schools of thought when it comes to the leadership of sheep, the Western view and the Eastern view. Shepherds in America follow the western philosophy.

Do you remember the television show "Rawhide" from the fifties and sixties? Maybe you remember Gil Favor, Rowdy Yates, and "Wishbone" the cook who drove the chuckwagon. "Rawhide" was a show about a cattle drive. The plot was basically the same every week for seven years, because every week I tuned in, they were still driving those cattle. I'm not sure they ever did get to where they were going.

The best thing about "Rawhide" was the opening song, sung by Frankie Laine. It was rough and tough with great orchestration and cracking bullwhips in the background. The song went something like this:

Keep 'em rollin' rollin' rollin'
Though the streams are swollen,
Keep them doggies rollin',
Rawhide!
No time to understand them,
Just ride and rope and brand 'em.

That's not good news if you are a doggie. Stop and think about it. No time to understand them, just ride and rope and brand them!

Western shepherds lead their sheep just like the cattle on "Rawhide." The western shepherd drives his sheep from behind, just like a cattle drive.

The Eastern shepherd in Palestine would never do that. The Eastern shepherd walks ahead of his sheep. They follow him, he doesn't follow them. That way, if danger is ahead, he meets it before the sheep do.

The good news is that we are not on a sheep drive. Christ is not driving you, He is leading you. We have a shepherd who does have time to understand us. Jesus Christ is out in front of us. Are you worried about the future? He is already in the future. Your future is secure. He is leading you. He certainly isn't driving you.

As the verse goes on, it further develops for us His style of leadership:

He leads me beside quiet waters.

My study about sheep uncovered something absolutely wild. Sheep are deathly afraid of running water. Thirsty sheep are so afraid of strong running water that they will die of thirst before they will drink from a rushing stream. Sheep are not sure-footed animals and they instinctively know they could easily slip as they try to drink from a furious current. If they fell in, their heavy coats of wool would soak up water in an instant and in seconds they would be dead.

The good Shepherd leads them beside quiet waters, or *stilled* waters.[2] The shepherd understands the fear of his sheep, so he will take some rocks and stones and divert some water safely away from the rushing stream. The shepherd constructs a small, safe inlet of water that is quiet and still. Then the sheep can drink without fear, for he has stilled the waters.

God has always been in the business of stilling the waters for his sheep. When the children of Israel left Egypt after hundreds of years of captivity, they suddenly found themselves between a rock and a hard place. The Red Sea lay in front of them while Pharaoh's pursuing army marched behind. There was no escape from either. But God stepped in and stilled the waters. He rolled back the sea and His people passed over on dry ground. He unstilled the waters at the appropriate moment and the enemies of His people drowned.

Do you remember when Jesus got into the boat with his disciples to cross the Sea of Galilee? Jesus was exhausted from a full day of ministry so he quickly went to sleep. Soon a storm started to brew on that calm sea and it quickly became a tempest. These guys had been on this water before and they had seen some pretty strong storms, but they had never seen anything like this. It got so bad they weren't sure they were going to make it. They had never been in waves like this. It looked as if their little boat would crack like a nut in the hands of a hungry man armed with a gleaming steel nutcracker.

As the storm worsened, they panicked. Feelings of anxiety and fear overwhelmed them. Terror and fright ruled the day. They rushed to the Lord, woke him out of his sleep, and screamed, "Lord, don't you care that we are perishing?"

Have you ever had that kind of experience? Perhaps life had been moving along peacefully when an unexpected phone call brought a raging storm into your life. You went from peace to panic in just seconds. A storm of circumstance threatened to overwhelm and engulf you. You prayed and prayed but it seemed as if the Shepherd were asleep. The storm got worse and you realized you weren't going to make it and you began to panic. Fear and anxiety seized your heart and quickened your heartbeat while simultaneously taking your breath away.

That's how the disciples felt. They woke up Jesus and said, "Lord, don't you care that we are perishing?" Jesus got up and spoke to the wind and waves. With a simple word He stilled the waters. Instantly it became quiet.

Sheep are afraid of torrents. The children of Israel panicked when they faced the Red Sea. The disciples panicked when they faced the Sea of Galilee. What is the raging water in your life? What is panicking you? Have you forgotten in the midst of your storm that you have a Shepherd who really does care? *Why then, you may be thinking, doesn't he still my waters?* The good news is this. He *will* still your waters and He will still them at exactly the right moment. You may get wet, you may even get soaked, but you will not drown. You have a Shepherd who will lead you beside stilled waters.

After Jesus calmed the storm, He looked at the disciples and asked, "Where is your faith?" Apparently they had left their faith on the shore. They needed their faith in the boat. If you are in a state of panic and anxiety, you may need to answer that same question: Where is your faith? Did you leave it at church? Have you lost it in some disastrous circumstances? Remember that you do not need a lot of faith. If you only have a little right now, that's OK. Just pull it out, dust it off, and put it in the hands of the Good Shepherd. You can trust Him. He hasn't forgotten you. He will quiet your storm. And He will do it at the right moment.

Do you know that great hymn of the church, "Jesus, I am panicking, panicking?" You probably don't. But perhaps you know a great hymn that says:

> Jesus, I am resting, resting,
> In the joy of what Thou art,
> I am finding out the greatness
> Of Thy loving heart.
> Thou hast bid me gaze upon Thee,
> And Thy beauty fills my soul,
> For by Thy transforming power,
> Thou hast made me whole.

Are you resting or are you panicking? Are you worshiping or are you worrying? You can't worship and worry at the same time. The antidote to worry is worship of the Great Shepherd. And worship always bring rest and refreshment into the life of His sheep.

THE SHEPHERD PROVIDES RESTORATION

It makes sense that the Shepherd provides rest and it makes sense that He would provide refreshment. But why does He provide restoration?

> He restores my soul,
> He guides me in the paths of righteousness
> For His name's sake.

Sheep need restoration because sheep have a tendency to stray. Sheep can be stubborn and strong-willed. Sheep can wander off the path the shepherd is blazing for them. When that happens the shepherd must restore them to the right path.

When a sheep wanders from the right path it is in tremendous danger. But sheep are stupid. They don't realize how much danger lurks out there. A wild beast can suddenly turn a sheep into lambchops. A sheep can take the wrong path and suddenly find itself on a precarious, rocky ledge. One false step and that sheep will become lambchops on the jagged rocks hundreds of feet below.

Every night at twilight, a good shepherd will count his sheep. If one sheep is missing, he will go and find that sheep before night falls. The shepherd knows what can happen to a wandering sheep during the night. So he will find the sheep and restore it to the flock.

Every once in a while, the shepherd will notice it's the same sheep who strays night after night. This little sheep is prone to wander, a very bad habit. After this happens several times in a short period, the shepherd will go looking for the sheep as usual, but on this evening he will do something unusual.

On this evening, the shepherd will find the little sheep, pick it up, and firmly hold it with one arm while positioning his strong staff against one of its legs. Then with a swift and strong motion, he will snap the sheep's leg with the staff. On this particular evening, the Shepherd breaks the leg of the little sheep.

Now, why would a loving, caring shepherd break the leg of a defenseless little sheep? How could such a committed shepherd do such a cruel thing? Haddon Robinson provides the answer:

> Back in the fold the shepherd makes a splint for the shattered leg and, during the days that follow, he carries that crippled sheep close to his heart. As the leg begins to mend, the shepherd sets the sheep down by his side. To the crippled animal, the smallest stream looms like a giant river, the tiniest knoll rises like a mountain. The sheep depends completely upon the shepherd to carry it across the terrain. After the leg has healed the sheep has learned a lesson: it must stay close to the shepherd's side.
>
> To break the leg of a poor, defenseless sheep seems almost vicious, unless you understand the shepherd's heart. Then you realize that what seems to be cruelty is really kindness. The shepherd knows that the sheep must remain close to him if it is to be protected from danger. So he breaks the leg, not to hurt it, but to restore it.[3]

Sometimes the only way God can break our legs is to break our hearts. It may be the loss of a child, the loss of a business, the loss of a marriage, the loss of a ministry, or the loss of our health. That too, seems almost cruel. But it's when our hearts are broken that we learn the lesson of staying close to the Shepherd. That is a lesson we *must* learn. For it is a jungle out there, a jungle of unrighteousness. He wants me on His path, the path of righteousness. The only way to stay on that path is to stay close to the Shepherd. That's why He will break your leg. That's why He will break your heart. He wants you to stay close to Him as you walk through life.

He has broken my leg. Perhaps he has broken yours. That's why spiritually speaking, I walk with a limp. Although it was painful, I'm glad He did it. Now I am mindful of staying close to the Shepherd. Most of us would not choose to have our legs broken. But that is much better than the alternative.

Who wants to be lambchops?

Notes

1. John MacArthur, *Our Sufficiency In Christ* (Dallas: Word, 1991), 141.

2. Haddon Robinson, *The Good Shepherd* (Chicago: Moody Press, 1968), 13. This excellent little book has been a primary source for many of the principles in this chapter.

3. Ibid., 16.

Chapter 9

Jungle Lambchops: The Sequel

The discontented man finds no easy chair.
Benjamin Franklin

A lot of people thought Bunky Knudsen was spoiled. He lived with his parents in a huge mansion, complete with servants and all the accompanying privileges of life among the upper crust. Bunky's father was president of General Motors and if there was any question about Bunky being spoiled, all doubt would have been erased by eavesdropping on a phone call between Bunky and his father.

It was the first day of summer vacation between Bunky's junior and senior year of high school. Bunky was sleeping in, as he planned to do all summer. But his father called about 8:00.

"Bunky," his father said, "how fast could you get down to the factory?"

"I could be there in about an hour," Bunky replied.

"Well, Son, I've got a gift for you. I'd like to give you a brand new 1927 Chevrolet."

"Dad, I'll be there in ten minutes."

When Bunky got down to the GM plant, his father took him past all the assembly lines to an old, dusty warehouse in the back corner of the GM property. He took out a key from his pocket, opened a rusty old padlock, and opened the double doors of the warehouse. There before Bunky's eyes was his brand new 1927 Chevrolet . . . in several thousand pieces.

Bunky Knudsen had a wise father. He knew that his son was spoiled and that it would be unwise for him to waste the months of summer. So Bunky suddenly was motivated to work from 7:00 in the morning until 10:00 or 11:00 each night. In his youthful excitement to assemble all the pieces of his new Chevy, something else was going on. Bunky was learning the car business from the ground up.

In my estimation, the three most feared words in the English language are: *some assembly required*. I have seen more than one Christmas Eve ruined as I scrambled late at night to assemble the pieces of an innocent looking toy. All it said on the box was: some assembly required. It should have said: some assembly required (plus an engineering degree from M.I.T.). The problem is, I didn't go to M.I.T. I went to M.I.C., K.E.Y.M.O.U.S.E.

God has given us everything we need to live the Christian life. But some assembly is required.

> So then, my beloved, just as you have always obeyed, not as in my presence only, but now much more in my absence, work our your salvation with fear and trembling; for it is God who is at work in you, both to will and to work for His good pleasure (Philippians 2:12-13, NASB).

We have a perfect Heavenly Father. He has given us a brand new Chevy, but we have to put some pieces together. This verse doesn't tell us to work *for* our salvation, but to work *out* our salvation. We work out what God has worked within. God works and we work. I can't fully comprehend all the ramifications of that truth, but it is clearly what the Bible teaches.

I find that in the Christian life I am not always sure how to work out the pieces so that they come together. That's precisely why I need a Shepherd. I'm a sheep and sheep are stupid. That's why we need a Shepherd to help us put together the pieces of life.

I'm supposed to put together some pieces. But without the Shepherd's help, I can fall to pieces. I need to be reminded that the Shepherd is right there with me as I walk through life. Whatever circumstances I face, he is there to help me put together the pieces.

THE SHEPHERD PROVIDES PROTECTION IN THE JUNGLE

Sheep have good reason to be afraid. As we have seen, they are defenseless. Defenseless sheep desperately need a strong shepherd.

> Even though I walk through the valley of the shadow of
> death,
> I fear no evil; for Thou art with me;
> Thy rod and Thy staff, they comfort me.

Psalm 23 is often used as a text to comfort a grieving family at a funeral service. Verse 4 has comforted countless families in countless generations. But the reference to the valley of the shadow of death is actually broader than it appears. H. C. Leupold, in his excellent commentary on the Psalms, comments that "the Hebrew word used contains no reference to death as such but does refer to all dark and bitter experiences, one of which may be death. So in the common use of the passage the thought of death need not be excluded, but the reference is certainly much broader."[1]

The Hebrew phrase could easily be rendered "even though I walk through the valley of deepest darkness." The death of a loved one is certainly a valley of deep darkness, but there are other valleys we face that can be incredibly dark. Whatever valley you are facing, the Shepherd will walk you through it.

None of us like to be in the dark. When we were kids, we usually wanted some kind of light left on so we could go to sleep. Kids are afraid of the dark. So are their parents. But parents are afraid of a different kind of dark. We are afraid of dark circumstances.

The problem with being in the dark is that you have no reference point. You don't know where you are. You have lost all perspective and all sense of direction. You hesitate to take a step because you don't know if you will land on terra firma or in the middle of thin air. We hate to be in the dark. It may be career, it may be a relationship, it may be our health. We don't like to be in the dark when it comes to any aspect of our lives.

There are times when we are in the dark. I already told you about my darkest time, but I didn't tell you the whole story. I trust that you won't mind if I supply a few more details. When Mary was pregnant with Josh, she had a bout with phlebitis. A blood clot had formed near her ankle, had broken loose, and was on its way to her heart when it lodged in her abdominal area. The doctor gave Mary some medicine to break down the clot and advised us not to get pregnant for at least a year. Otherwise she could easily be in the hospital for months.

So we were shocked when Mary turned up pregnant several months later. We couldn't believe she was pregnant. We were living from day to day on pins and needles to see if she would make it through another week without going to the hospital. With two children under the age of five it was difficult for her to not overdo it.

What was really tough was when Mary returned from the doctor to report he had strongly urged her to abort. According to the doctor, the medication Mary had been taking to break down the clot (when she didn't realize she was pregnant) had probably adversely affected our baby. He told Mary the chances were very good we would have a deformed child. In fact, he predicted we would have "a little monster." What a great bedside manner this guy had!

It was a time of great darkness for us. But let me tell you the good news. Josh was born and he was perfect. He could have been born handicapped and still he would have been a gift from God. In a theological sense, all of us are born handicapped. But some children also have a physical handicap. God was gracious to us in that Josh was born without any physical defects whatsoever.

Mary never spent a day in the hospital other than the day she delivered Josh. There was no further clotting and there was no hemorrhaging. Everything went perfectly.

But I will never forget the night I woke up at 3:00 A.M. in a cold sweat. The pillow was soaked from my perspiration. I had dreamed that Mary hadn't made it through the delivery. In my dream she started to hemorrhage right after delivering and the doctors could not counter quickly enough to effectively clot the hemorrhage. She died. I was left with three kids under five. Then I woke up.

I have to tell you I was panicked by what might be. And remember, I didn't know the end of the story. We were still walking through it. I couldn't see the next step and neither could

Mary. Neither could the doctors. They were doing the best they could, but they had never been in this situation. Things were very dark and I was very afraid. But the Good Shepherd walked *with* us through every step of that dark valley. He didn't take us around the valley, He didn't tunnel us under it, He didn't fly us over it. He took us *through* the valley of deep darkness. He will take you through your valley as well.

There was more than one moment when I felt like panicking. But during this time I read a gold mine of a book by Dr. Martyn Lloyd-Jones titled *Spiritual Depression*. In that book so full of biblical wisdom and insight, Lloyd-Jones offered a definition of faith I had never heard. He said faith is a refusal to panic. I love that definition. I think it hits the nail on the head.

The reason you can walk through the valley of deep darkness and not panic is that the Shepherd is walking with you. You can't see in the dark, but He can. The dark doesn't have to overwhelm you. You don't have to panic. You refuse to panic because of the presence of the Shepherd. If he wasn't there you would have every reason to panic. But He *is* there. You don't have to fear any evil lurking in the dark.

He carries with him a rod and a staff. You can't see Him and you can't see his rod and staff, but He is there and so are the rod and staff. They are there for your protection. That's why David says "Thy rod and Thy staff, they comfort me." I don't think the emphasis of that verse is "Thy *rod* and Thy *staff*, they comfort me." I think the emphasis is "*Thy* rod and *Thy* staff, they comfort me." David's comfort doesn't come from any old rod or staff; his comfort comes from the rod and staff being in the right hands, the Shepherd's hands. That's why you will be protected and that's why you don't have to be terrorized by any evil, no matter how dark it is. Your Shepherd can not only see in the dark, He owns the dark.

The Shepherd Provides Food In The Jungle

Sheep have to eat and keeping them in abundant grass is a full-time job for the shepherd. While the sheep are grazing on the good green grass of a meadow, the shepherd must already be thinking of where the next meal will come from.

Thou dost prepare a table before me . . . (Psalm 23:5a).

Margaret Laird was wondering where the next meal was going to come from. Not for herself, but for her new baby boy, Clifford. Margaret believed her infant was going to need some special meals, but these special meals were virtually impossible to get. It was 1931, and Margaret and her husband had left the United States to serve their second term as missionaries in Africa. Margaret describes the situation in her own words:

> Foodwise, we weren't ready for Clifford. Going back to Africa the first time with Lawrence (her husband) and Arlene (her duaghter), and with Marian on the way, I had taken some oatmeal with me as well as prunes. But a missionary lady came to Ippy after we'd settled in. I delivered her baby and took care of her for over a year . . . She had a bottle baby, so I used up my supply of oatmeal and prunes for her baby.
>
> Clifford came along and found us without any of those items. He also was a bottle baby and was not getting along very well on goat's milk. I wanted oatmeal water to dilute the goat's milk. We had no oranges at that time.
>
> I had lost my first baby, and I always thought it was because I gave her orange juice from fruit not fully ripe. I do not know, but in any case I wanted to give Clifford the prune juice.[2]

Margaret obviously had good reasons for wanting this special provision for her baby. But she wasn't in America where she could easily get oatmeal and prunes for her baby. She was in the middle of Africa.

> This same woman [whom she had previously cared for] stopped by to visit. She and her family were on their way to Bambari, our main station seventy-five miles away, to get supplies, and she had offered to shop for us. The woman was looking over my shopping list, on which I had put oatmeal and prunes.
>
> She looked rather reprovingly and said, "Now, that's silly."
>
> I was rather taken aback.
>
> "You knew you were going to have a baby. You should have ordered those things from America. You know good and well I'll never find those things at Bambari."
>
> I couldn't believe my ears. I had returned from America prepared, but I had given all my oatmeals and prunes to *her* baby.[3]

Margaret was so upset by the insensitivity of this woman that she couldn't speak. The family left for their shopping trip, but Margaret was devastated by the calloused attack of the woman. She had taken care of her friend's baby, giving it the oatmeal and prunes that her baby now needed. The woman was right about one thing. Oatmeal and prunes were not to be found in the middle of Africa in 1931. Margaret went to the bedroom to pour out her heart to the Lord.

> Lord, you know all about it. If it's presumptuous, then show me and forgive me. But you are able to provide for my children in the heart of Africa, and You know I had no money to order these things. You know I have never asked anybody to send me anything. If You are able to provide, You provide the things my children need.
>
> I was still on my knees when my husband called me. I didn't pay attention at first. He called again. I got up and went out.[4]

Her husband introduced her to two men from a Portuguese mining camp far to the north. They had driven the long distance to talk with Margaret's husband. A young Belgian miner had recently died of sunstroke, and his very last request was that he might be buried at Ippy. He had recently come to know Christ through reading some printed material from the little mission station where Margaret and her family lived. This was the reason for their visit and soon the arrangements were made.

> The message delivered, the Portuguese got up to go to the car. I accompanied them to the veranda.
>
> One of them said rather nervously, "Mrs. Laird, I wonder if you would be insulted if I offered you something for the children."
>
> "Why, not at all. I would think it was your graciousness and God's provision."
>
> "Well, you know we get all of our provisions from Belgium. We get two big wooden crates each month. I don't know what they think we are, but every month they send us tins of oatmeal, dried prunes, and cocoa that none of us ever use. I happen to have mine with me. Would you accept them?"[5]

Margaret Laird was shocked. God had the answer on the way before she even made her request. For the rest of their time on the mission field, every month she would receive, like clockwork, ten to twelve tins of oatmeal and dried prunes. Her baby,

Clifford, grew strong and healthy through the unique provisions sent special delivery by the Good Shepherd.

Psalm 23:5 goes on to indicate that Jesus Christ cannot only supply whatever it is we need, wherever we need it (even oatmeal and prunes to Africa), but that he will feed us even in the midst of enemies and threatening circumstances:

> Thou dost prepare a table before me in the presence of my enemies (Psalm 23:5).

A good shepherd never sets the sheep loose on a new field without first carefully evaluating it. The shepherd knows what the sheep don't. Not every inviting field is harmless.

> The shepherd inspects the [new] field closely, walking up and down the field looking for grass that could poison the sheep. He also inspects the field for vipers. These tiny brown adders live under the ground, and they have a way of popping up out of their small holes and nipping the noses of the sheep. Their bite is poisonous, and sometimes the inflammation from their bite will kill the sheep.
>
> The shepherd leaves the sheep outside any such infested field. Then he walks up and down the field until he finds the vipers' holes. He takes from his girdle a bottle of thick oil. Then, raking over any long grass with his staff, he pours a circle of oil at the top of every viper's hole he can find. As he leads the sheep into the field, he anoints the head of each sheep with the oil. When the vipers beneath the ground realize that the sheep are grazing above, they come out of their holes to do their deadly damage. But the oil keeps them from getting out. The smooth bodies of the vipers cannot pass over the slippery oil, and they are prisoners inside their own holes . . . literally, therefore, the sheep are allowed to graze in the presence of their enemies.[6]

With that background in mind, the familiar words of Psalm 23:5 take on even greater significance:

> Thou dost prepare a table before me in the presence of my
>   enemies;
>   Thou hast anointed my head with oil;

Let me ask you a question. Who are your enemies? Who's trying to get you in your jungle? Is someone at work talking behind your back to your boss? Or when you took your current position, were you promised certain things if your performance reviews were high? Well, the reviews are in and you're doing well, but your superior has conveniently forgotten his promise—and it never was put down in writing.

Is someone trying to erode your reputation? Is someone a constant irritant and a source of discouragement? Is someone trying to pull a power-play on you? Is someone perpetually bugging you? Unless I miss my guess, there probably is someone like that. We all get bugged. Especially sheep. They get so bugged they can't even eat.

> Sheep, in summer, become frantic in their attempts to escape nose flies. They will run, they will toss their heads, they will try to hide in the brush, they will stamp their feet, they will refuse to graze. Both the ewes and the lambs will stop eating, go off milking, lose weight, and stop growing.
>
> Only the strictest attention to the behavior of the sheep can forestall the difficulties of "fly time." At the very first sign of flies among the flock he will apply an antidote to the heads.

The application of this remedy would cause an incredible transformation.

> Once the oil had been applied to the sheep's head there was an immediate change in behavior. Gone was the aggravation; gone the frenzy; gone the irritability and the restlessness. Instead, the sheep would start to feed quietly again, then soon lie down in peaceful contentment.[7]

In Psalm 27, David says:

The Lord is my light and my salvation;
>   Whom shall I fear?
>   The Lord is the defense of my life;
>   Whom shall I dread?

Kids with big brothers always have an advantage. If you give a kid like that a hard time, inevitably you are going to deal with his big brother. We have an Elder Brother (to use the scriptural term) who is also a Shepherd. To be more precise, He is The Shepherd. An Almighty Shepherd. An Omnipotent Shepherd who controls everything in your life—including your enemies.

THE SHEPHERD PROVIDES WATER IN THE JUNGLE

There is a difference between a shepherd and a hired hand. In days of summer and drought, water sometimes isn't easy to find. That means the shepherd must quench the sheep's thirst from a well.

> Sometimes a shepherd found a very deep well from which to draw water for his flock. Many were a hundred feet down to the water. To draw the water the shepherd used a long rope with a leather bucket at the end. The bucket held only three quarts. It had to be let down and drawn up hand over hand and the water poured into large stone cups beside the well. It was a long, laborious process. If a shepherd had one hundred sheep, he might have to draw for two hours if he allowed the sheep to drink all they wished.[8]

The hired hand would never fill the stone cup to overflowing. He might fill it halfway, but not to the top. The work was just too taxing in the pounding, Palestinian sun. That's why the sheep need a shepherd instead of a hired hand. The Shepherd not only provides for the sheep, but he cares for the sheep. And the fact that He cares affects the quality and extent of his provision.

Earlier I suggested that every family needs two things: provision and care. There is no greater model of provision and care than Jesus Christ. He has both in perfect balance. Because He cares for us He provides cups for us that overflow. What a model for a husband and wife as they raise a family in the jungle!

THE SHEPHERD PROVIDES CONTENTMENT IN THE JUNGLE

The sheep is getting ready to make his summary statement in verse 6. Two points must be reinforced about the greatness of the Shepherd:

> Surely goodness and mercy will follow me all the days of my
> life,
> And I will dwell in the house of the Lord forever.

The first statement is a statement of contentment. That is a rare thing in our society. A number of people are successful, a number of people are famous, a number of people are wealthy, but very, very few are content.

Everyone has heard of Ernest Hemingway. Joe Aldrich paints

this portrait of Hemingway:

> Ernest Hemingway's great passion was to be a successful writer. And so he was. He collected as proof of his success both the Pulitzer and Nobel prizes. His book *The Old Man and the Sea* made him wealthy and famous. He was free to do whatever his heart desired: do whatever he wanted, travel wherever his whims directed. He sought excitement and adventure; he was much married and divorced.
>
> But apparently neither fame nor fortune satisfied. He came to his sunset years and, like countless others, added up his life, looked at the final figures, and concluded it was futile and not worth continuing. His suicide sent shock waves throughout the world.[9]

Hemingway had everything. He could buy anything or do anything. Yet he was missing one critical ingredient: contentment.

People everywhere are looking for satisfaction and contentment. In the eighties it was believed contentment would come with living the good life. Contentment would come if you could afford a Rolex instead of a Timex, if you got into a BMW instead of a Honda. But people began to realize that contentment can't be found by acquiring more things. As a result, there seems to be a national turn among baby-boomers back to the simple life. At least that's the trend that *Time* magazine is noticing.

Last Sunday evening I picked up the April 8, 1991, issue of *Time*. The cover story caught my eye: "The Simple Life: Rejecting the rat race, Americans get back to basics." The inside story began like this: "Goodbye to having it all. Tired of trendiness and materialism, Americans are rediscovering the joys of home life, basic values and things that last."

That sounds like a step in the right direction, doesn't it? The article then cites several examples of people returning to the simple life. In the 1980s . . .

- Karen Glance, an apparel-industry executive, used to travel on business almost every day. Home was where she repacked her suitcase. Now she operates a food market in her St. Paul neighborhood. "I'm tired at night, but it's a healthy tired."
- Barry Blake, a liquor-industry executive, was living lavishly in a Manhattan penthouse and scrambling up the career ladder. Now Blake runs an apple winery and cider mill in Vermont.

"The old corporate chase doesn't mean anything anymore."

- Peter Lynch built the largest stock mutual fund in the country, worth $13 billion. But he had no time to spend with his children. At forty-six, he quit. Now, instead of picking stocks from dawn to dusk, Lynch gets up early to make peanut-butter sandwiches for his three daughters.

I think each of these people should be commended. They are making healthy adjustments to their lives. Like Hemingway, they have discovered that contentment doesn't come with success, so they are going back to the simple life.

The problem is that contentment can't be found in the simple life, either. Maybe that's what Americans will spend the nineties searching for. They will be looking for contentment in the simple life because they couldn't find it in the "good" life. But the problem is that contentment *cannot* be found without knowing the Shepherd. Jesus Christ is the door to contentment, and without Him you can't get there from here.

Contentment is the byproduct of following the Shepherd. It is experiencing the inner-peace that only He can provide. It is knowing He will promote you at the right time. Contentment is the sense of satisfaction that comes to a husband and wife as they emulate the provision and care of the Shepherd to their own children. Contentment comes from serving Christ instead of money and from providing not only financially for your family, but emotionally, morally and spiritually.

Contentment is not passivity. Contentment is not complacency. It doesn't mean you lack drive or ambition. It does mean you channel your drive and ambition in a way that pleases the Lord.

Contentment requires another critical element: it demands that you look at life through a wide-angle lens.

I have a 35mm camera. It came in a case with three lenses. Now, I am no camera buff. I bought this camera back when our first child, Rachel, was born. I am a novice when it comes to cameras. All I know how to do is to change lenses, focus, and snap the picture. But I really like those three lenses.

One lens is called the normal lens. With that lens on the camera, I look through the viewfinder and see everything normally, just as I would with my naked eye. It's a normal lens.

Another lens is called a telephoto. It's longer and narrower than the normal lens, and when it's on the camera I can stand in exactly the same spot and focus on a bird's nest seventy-five yards away. I'm standing in the same place, but now the only thing I see is the bird's nest. Everything else is shut out.

A third lens is called the wide-angle. When I stand in exactly the same spot and switch to the wide-angle, my perspective completely changes. For now instead of focusing on one object or seeing things normally, I am looking at a broad panorama. I am now seeing the big picture.

When David says "surely goodness and mercy will follow me *all* the days of my life," he is looking at life through a wide-angle lens. When hardships and difficulties come into our lives, we tend to pull out the telephoto lens. All we can see is the disappointment, and it doesn't seem as if goodness and mercy are following us. That's why we can't forget the wide-angle lens. When we look at the big picture, it all adds up. Goodness and mercy are following us because the Shepherd is leading us. That's the key to contentment—or, more precisely, it's *part* of the key to contentment.

THE SHEPHERD LEADS US HOME

The second aspect that brings contentment is knowing *where* the Shepherd is leading us. That's why the wide-angle lens is so important. It doesn't just take in life on earth, but it pulls eternity into view.

And I will dwell in the house of the LORD forever. (Psalm 23:6).

May I ask you a question? Who is number one in your heart? Who calls the shots in your life? Is Jesus Christ the Shepherd of your heart? If you have given your life to Christ, then I have some great news for you. You are going to be in the presence of the Shepherd forever.

See, we are on a journey. Jesus Christ is leading us through this life and this jungle. He will lead you through every trial, every hardship, every disappointment, and every set of confusing circumstances. He knows what He is doing with you every single moment and He always knows where you are. He also knows where He is taking you. Jesus Christ is leading you to heaven. And if He is the Shepherd of your heart, if He is your Lord and Savior, your arrival is guaranteed.

J. Vernon McGee pointed out that a shepherd who embarked on a long journey with a flock of sheep was considered successful if he arrived with more than 50 percent of his sheep.[10] The dangers to sheep were monumental. Disease, poison grass, torrential water, and wild animals were just a few of the things that killed sheep on a lengthy sojourn.

However, Jesus Christ is like no other shepherd. And as Dr. McGee put it, "When the Lord—who is the Great Shepherd of the Sheep, the Good Shepherd of the Sheep, and Chief Shepherd of the Sheep—starts out with one hundred sheep, He's going to come home with one hundred sheep; He will not lose one of them."[11]

The good news is that Jesus Christ has never lost a sheep. He was emphatic about that when He said, "My sheep hear my voice, and I know them, and they follow me; and I give eternal life to them, and they shall never perish; and no one shall snatch them out of My hand. My Father, who has given them to Me, is greater than all; and no one is able to snatch them out of the Father's hand" (John 10:27-29).

When it comes to His sheep, Jesus Christ is very serious. That's why you can be content in your jungle. You have a Shepherd and He knows where He is going. He is taking you with Him.

Do you know what contentment is? It is tagging along next to the Shepherd as you walk through your jungle. That's why contentment is possible even when your circumstances aren't so great. Even when it looks like you won't make it, you *will* make it. The Lord is your Shepherd. That's why you will make it through the jungle.

Sheep aren't cut out to survive in the jungle. We all know that. But your Shepherd is Lord of the Jungle. That's why in our home, in our jungle, we like to listen to Sandi Patti sing these words:

> Maker of this heart of mine, you know me very well,

You understand my deepest part more than I know myself.
So when I face the darkness, when I need to find my way,
I'll trust in you, Shepherd of my heart.

Keeper of this heart of mine, your patience has no end,
You've loved me back into your arms, time and time again.
So if I start to wander, like a lamb that's gone astray,
I'll trust in you, Shepherd of my heart.

Giver of this life in me, you're what I'm living for,
For all my deepest gratitude, you love me even more.
So as I walk through valleys, listening for the Master's call,
I'll trust in you, Shepherd of my heart.[12]

That's the theme song of *Better Homes and Jungles*. And you can begin to sing it the moment you give Him your heart.

Notes

1. H. C. Leupold, *Psalms* (Grand Rapids: Baker, n.d.), 213.

2. Margaret Laird, *They Called Me Mama* (Chicago: Moody Press, 1975), 78.

3. Ibid.

4. Ibid.

5. Ibid.

6. Charles W. Slemming, cited by Haddon Robinson, *The Good Shepherd* (Chicago: Moody Press, 1968), 25.

7. Don Baker, *The Way of the Shepherd* (Portland, Ore.: Multnomah Press, 1987), 27.

8. Ibid.

9. Joseph C. Aldrich, *Satisfaction: Investing In What Is Important To God* (Portland, Ore.: Multnomah Press, 1983), 3.

10. J. Vernon McGee, *Thru The Bible*, Volume IV, (Nashville: Thomas Nelson, 1983), 706.

11. Ibid., 706.

12. "Shepherd of My Heart," words and music by Mark Baldwin and Dick Tunney, Copyright 1984, Laurel Press, a div. of Lorenz Creative Services/Pamela Kay Music/Charlie Monk Music, Nashville, TN. Used by permission.